Interactive Notebooks
LANGUAGE ARTS

Grade 2

Credits

Content Editors: Elise Craver, Christine Schwab, Angela Triplett

Visit *carsondellosa.com* for correlations to Common Core, state, national, and Canadian provincial standards.

Carson-Dellosa Publishing LLC
PO Box 35665
Greensboro, NC 27425 USA
carsondellosa.com

978-1-4838-2469-7
03-162187784

Table of Contents

© Carson-Dellosa • CD-104653

What Are Interactive Notebooks?

Interactive notebooks are a unique form of note taking. Teachers guide students through creating pages of notes on new topics. Instead of being in the traditional linear, handwritten format, notes are colorful and spread across the pages. Notes also often include drawings, diagrams, and 3-D elements to make the material understandable and relevant. Students are encouraged to complete their notebook pages in ways that make sense to them. With this personalization, no two pages are exactly the same.

Because of their creative nature, interactive notebooks allow students to be active participants in their own learning. Teachers can easily differentiate pages to address the levels and needs of each learner. The notebooks are arranged sequentially, and students can create tables of contents as they create pages, making it simple for students to use their notebooks for reference throughout the year. The interactive, easily personalized format makes interactive notebooks ideal for engaging students in learning new concepts.

Using interactive notebooks can take as much or as little time as you like. Students will initially take longer to create pages but will get faster as they become familiar with the process of creating pages. You may choose to only create a notebook page as a class at the beginning of each unit, or you may choose to create a new page for each topic within a unit. You can decide what works best for your students and schedule.

A student's interactive notebook for long and short vowel sounds

Getting Started

You can start using interactive notebooks at any point in the school year. Use the following guidelines to help you get started in your classroom. (For more specific details, management ideas, and tips, see page 10.)

1. Plan each notebook.

Use the planning template (page 9) to lay out a general plan for the topics you plan to cover in each notebook for the year.

2. Choose a notebook type.

Interactive notebooks are usually either single-subject, spiral-bound notebooks, composition books, or three-ring binders with loose-leaf paper. Each type presents pros and cons. See page 5 for a more in-depth look at each type of notebook.

3. Allow students to personalize their notebooks.

Have students decorate their notebook covers, as well as add their names and subjects. This provides a sense of ownership and emphasizes the personalized nature of the notebooks.

4. Number the pages and create the table of contents.

Have students number the bottom outside corner of each page, front and back. When completing a new page, adding a table of contents entry will be easy. Have students title the first page of each notebook "Table of Contents." Have them leave several blank pages at the front of each notebook for the table of contents. Refer to your general plan for an idea of about how many entries students will be creating.

5. Start creating pages.

Always begin a new page by adding an entry to the table of contents. Create the first notebook pages along with students to model proper format and expectations.

This book contains individual topics for you to introduce. Use the pages in the order that best fits your curriculum. You may also choose to alter the content presented to better match your school's curriculum. The provided lesson plans often do not instruct students to add color. Students should make their own choices about personalizing the content in a way that makes sense to them. Encourage students to highlight and color the pages as they desire while creating them.

After introducing topics, you may choose to add more practice pages. Use the reproducibles (pages 78–96) to easily create new notebook pages for practice or to introduce topics not addressed in this book.

Use the grading rubric (page 11) to grade students' interactive notebooks at various points throughout the year. Provide students copies of the rubric to glue into their notebooks and refer to as they create pages.

What Type of Notebook Should I Use?

Spiral Notebook

The pages in this book are formatted for a standard one-subject notebook.

Pros

- Notebook can be folded in half.
- Page size is larger.
- It is inexpensive.
- It often comes with pockets for storing materials.

Cons

- Pages can easily fall out.
- Spirals can snag or become misshapen.
- Page count and size vary widely.
- It is not as durable as a binder.

Tips

- Encase the spiral in duct tape to make it more durable.
- Keep the notebooks in a central place to prevent them from getting damaged in desks.

Composition Notebook

Pros

- Pages don't easily fall out.
- Page size and page count are standard.
- It is inexpensive.

Cons

- Notebook cannot be folded in half.
- Page size is smaller.
- It is not as durable as a binder.

Tips

- Copy pages meant for standard-sized notebooks at 85 or 90 percent. Test to see which works better for your notebook.

Binder with Loose-Leaf Paper

Pros

- Pages can be easily added, moved, or removed.
- Pages can be removed individually for grading.
- You can add full-page printed handouts.
- It has durable covers.

Cons

- Pages can easily fall out.
- Pages aren't durable.
- It is more expensive than a notebook.
- Students can easily misplace or lose pages.
- Larger size makes it more difficult to store.

Tips

- Provide hole reinforcers for damaged pages.

How to Organize an Interactive Notebook

You may organize an interactive notebook in many different ways. You may choose to organize it by unit and work sequentially through the book. Or, you may choose to create different sections that you will revisit and add to throughout the year. Choose the format that works best for your students and subject.

An interactive notebook includes different types of pages in addition to the pages students create. Non-content pages you may want to add include the following:

Title Page

This page is useful for quickly identifying notebooks. It is especially helpful in classrooms that use multiple interactive notebooks for different subjects. Have students write the subject (such as "Language Arts") on the title page of each interactive notebook. They should also include their full names. You may choose to have them include other information such as the teacher's name, classroom number, or class period.

Table of Contents

The table of contents is an integral part of the interactive notebook. It makes referencing previously created pages quick and easy for students. Make sure that students leave several pages at the beginning of each notebook for a table of contents.

Expectations and Grading Rubric

It is helpful for each student to have a copy of the expectations for creating interactive notebook pages. You may choose to include a list of expectations for parents and students to sign, as well as a grading rubric (page 11).

Unit Title Pages

Consider using a single page at the beginning of each section to separate it. Title the page with the unit name. Add a tab (page 78) to the edge of the page to make it easy to flip to the unit. Add a table of contents for only the pages in that unit.

Glossary

Reserve a six-page section at the back of the notebook where students can create a glossary. Draw a line to split in half the front and back of each page, creating 24 sections. Combine Q and R and Y and Z to fit the entire alphabet. Have students add an entry as each new vocabulary word is introduced.

Formatting Student Notebook Pages

The other major consideration for planning an interactive notebook is how to treat the left and right sides of a notebook spread. Interactive journals are usually viewed with the notebook open flat. This creates a left side and a right side. You have several options for how to treat the two sides of the spread.

Traditionally, the right side is used for the teacher-directed part of the lesson, and the left side is used for students to interact with the lesson content. The lessons in this book use this format. However, you may prefer to switch the order for your class so that the teacher-directed learning is on the left and the student input is on the right.

It can also be important to include standards, learning objectives, or essential questions in interactive notebooks. You may choose to write these on the top-left side of each page before completing the teacher-directed page on the right side. You may also choose to have students include the "Introduction" part of each lesson in that same top-left section. This is the *in, through, out* method. Students enter *in* the lesson on the top left of the page, go *through* the lesson on the right page, and exit *out* of the lesson on the bottom left with a reflection activity.

The following chart details different types of items and activities that you could include on each side.

Left Side Student Output	Right Side Teacher-Directed Learning
• learning objectives • essential questions • I Can statements • brainstorming • making connections • summarizing • making conclusions • practice problems • opinions • questions • mnemonics • drawings and diagrams	• vocabulary and definitions • mini-lessons • folding activities • steps in a process • example problems • notes • diagrams • graphic organizers • hints and tips • big ideas

Planning for the Year

Making a general plan for interactive notebooks will help with planning, grading, and testing throughout the year. You do not need to plan every single page, but knowing what topics you will cover and in what order can be helpful in many ways.

Use the Interactive Notebook Plan (page 9) to plan your units and topics and where they should be placed in the notebooks. Remember to include enough pages at the beginning for the non-content pages, such as the title page, table of contents, and grading rubric. You may also want to leave a page at the beginning of each unit to place a mini table of contents for just that section.

In addition, when planning new pages, it can be helpful to sketch the pieces you will need to create. Use the following notebook template and notes to plan new pages.

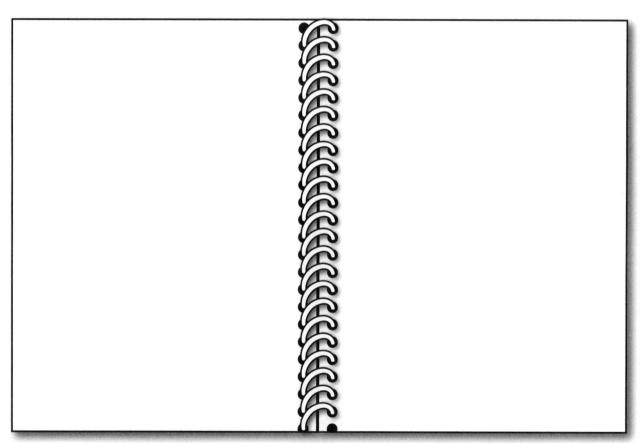

Left Side   **Right Side**

Notes

_____

_____

_____

Interactive Notebook Plan

Page	Topic	Page	Topic
1		51	
2		52	
3		53	
4		54	
5		55	
6		56	
7		57	
8		58	
9		59	
10		60	
11		61	
12		62	
13		63	
14		64	
15		65	
16		66	
17		67	
18		68	
19		69	
20		70	
21		71	
22		72	
23		73	
24		74	
25		75	
26		76	
27		77	
28		78	
29		79	
30		80	
31		81	
32		82	
33		83	
34		84	
35		85	
36		86	
37		87	
38		88	
39		89	
40		90	
41		91	
42		92	
43		93	
44		94	
45		95	
46		96	
47		97	
48		98	
49		99	
50		100	

Managing Interactive Notebooks in the Classroom

Working with Younger Students

- Use your yearly plan to preprogram a table of contents that you can copy and give to students to glue into their notebooks, instead of writing individual entries.

- Have assistants or parent volunteers precut pieces.

- Create glue sponges to make gluing easier. Place large sponges in plastic containers with white glue. The sponges will absorb the glue. Students can wipe the backs of pieces across the sponges to apply the glue with less mess.

Creating Notebook Pages

- For storing loose pieces, add a pocket to the inside back cover. Use the envelope pattern (page 81), an envelope, or a resealable plastic bag. Or, tape the bottom and side edges of the two last pages of the notebook together to create a large pocket.

- When writing under flaps, have students trace the outline of each flap so that they can visualize the writing boundary.

- Where the dashed line will be hidden on the inside of the fold, have students first fold the piece in the opposite direction so that they can see the dashed line. Then, students should fold the piece back the other way along the same fold line to create the fold in the correct direction.

- To avoid losing pieces, have students keep all of their scraps on their desks until they have finished each page.

- To contain paper scraps and avoid multiple trips to the trash can, provide small groups with small buckets or tubs.

- For students who run out of room, keep full and half sheets available. Students can glue these to the bottom of the pages and fold them up when not in use.

Dealing with Absences

- Create a model notebook for absent students to reference when they return to school.

- Have students cut a second set of pieces as they work on their own pages.

Using the Notebook

- To organize sections of the notebook, provide each student with a sheet of tabs (page 78).

- To easily find the next blank page, either cut off the top-right corner of each page as it is used or attach a long piece of yarn or ribbon to the back cover to be used as a bookmark.

Interactive Notebook Grading Rubric

4

_____ Table of contents is complete.

_____ All notebook pages are included.

_____ All notebook pages are complete.

_____ Notebook pages are neat and organized.

_____ Information is correct.

_____ Pages show personalization, evidence of learning, and original ideas.

3

_____ Table of contents is mostly complete.

_____ One notebook page is missing.

_____ Notebook pages are mostly complete.

_____ Notebook pages are mostly neat and organized.

_____ Information is mostly correct.

_____ Pages show some personalization, evidence of learning, and original ideas.

2

_____ Table of contents is missing a few entries.

_____ A few notebook pages are missing.

_____ A few notebook pages are incomplete.

_____ Notebook pages are somewhat messy and unorganized.

_____ Information has several errors.

_____ Pages show little personalization, evidence of learning, or original ideas.

1

_____ Table of contents is incomplete.

_____ Many notebook pages are missing.

_____ Many notebook pages are incomplete.

_____ Notebook pages are too messy and unorganized to use.

_____ Information is incorrect.

_____ Pages show no personalization, evidence of learning, or original ideas.

Long and Short Vowel Sounds

Introduction

Review the definition of a long vowel sound as a vowel that says its name. Then, review the short vowel sound for each vowel. Provide each student with a self-stick note with a one- or two-syllable word written on it. Have students read their words and circle the vowel sounds. Draw two large circles on the board and label them *short vowels* and *long vowels*. Have students bring their words to the board and place them into the correct circles. As a class, review the words to determine if the students placed the words in the circles correctly.

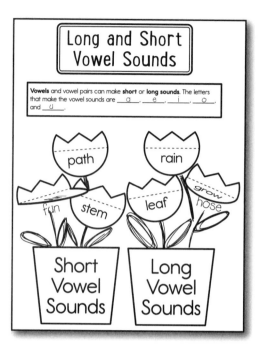

Creating the Notebook Page

Guide students through the following steps to complete the right-hand page in their notebooks.

1. Add a Table of Contents entry for the Long and Short Vowel Sounds pages.

2. Cut out the title and glue it to the top of the page.

3. Cut out the *vowels and vowel pairs can make* piece and glue it below the title. Complete the definition of a vowel by filling in the blanks. (The letters that make the vowel sounds are **a**, **e**, **i**, **o**, and **u**.)

4. Cut out the flowerpot pieces and glue them to the bottom of the page.

5. Cut out the flower flaps. Read the word on each flap and decide if it contains a short or a long vowel sound. Then, apply glue to the back of the top section and attach it above the correct flowerpot, leaving enough room to draw a stem to connect it to the flowerpot.

6. Under each flap, write another word with the same vowel sound.

Reflect on Learning

To complete the left-hand page, have students draw two large flowers with five petals each. Have students label the centers of the flowers *short* and *long*. Then, have students write words with short and long vowel sounds in the petals on each flower.

Long and Short Vowel Sounds

Vowels and vowel pairs can make **short** or **long sounds**. The letters that make the vowel sounds are _____, _____, _____, _____, and _____.

rain

stem

grow

sun

path

leaf

Short Vowel Sounds

Long Vowel Sounds

R-Controlled Vowels

Introduction

Explain that when the letter *r* follows a vowel, the vowel sound changes. The new sound is neither short nor long. It makes one of the following "bossy r" sounds: *ar, er, ir, or,* and *ur.* Write a few examples of *r*-controlled words on the board such as *barn, firm,* and *storm.* Explain that the *r* is bossy and controls how each vowel sound is pronounced. Say the words together. Then, program construction paper stars with *r*-controlled vowel words, omitting the bossy *r* sounds. For example, write *f__m* for *farm.* Provide each student with a star. Then, have them fill in the blanks with an *r*-controlled vowel sound to form a complete word. Have students share their words.

R-Controlled Vowels

Creating the Notebook Page

Guide students through the following steps to complete the right-hand page in their notebooks.

1. Add a Table of Contents entry for the *R*-Controlled Vowels pages.

2. Cut out the title and glue it to the top of the page.

3. Cut out the flap book. Cut on the solid lines to create five flaps. Apply glue to the back of the left section and attach it to the page.

4. Cut out the picture cards. Write the consonants that would complete the word for the picture on each card. Read the word. Glue each word under the correct flap.

5. Write another *r*-controlled vowel word with the same spelling pattern on the back of each flap.

Reflect on Learning

To complete the left-hand page, have students draw five stars. Then, students should write one *r*-controlled vowel word in each star. Have students highlight letters that make the *r*-controlled vowel sound in each word.

When a vowel is followed by an **r**, it makes a different sound.

ar

er

ir

or

ur

___ ir

___ er

___ ar

___ ur

___ or

___ ur

___ or

___ ir

___ ar

___ er

Beginning Consonant Digraphs

Students will need a brass paper fastener to complete this page.

Introduction

Write several *ch-*, *sh-*, *th-*, and *wh-* beginning consonant digraph words on the board. Say the words aloud. Explain that a consonant digraph combines two consonant sounds to make a new sound. Discuss how the consonant digraph produces the new sound at the beginning in these words. Ask students to give more examples of words with beginning consonant digraphs. Write them on the board as the students say them. Have volunteers come to the board and underline the beginning consonant digraph in each word.

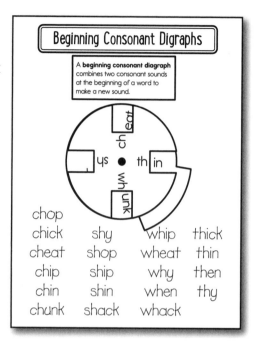

Creating the Notebook Page

Guide students through the following steps to complete the right-hand page in their notebooks.

1. Add a Table of Contents entry for the Beginning Consonant Digraphs pages.

2. Cut out the title and glue it to the top of the page.

3. Cut out the definition piece and glue it below the title. Discuss what a beginning consonant digraph is.

4. Cut out the three circles. Place the digraph circle on top of the ending sounds circle and then place the smallest circle on the bottom with the gray side down. Push a brass paper fastener through the dot at the center to connect the circles. (It may be helpful to create the hole in each piece separately first.) Apply glue to the gray glue section and attach it below the definition piece. Both circles should spin freely. Do not press the brass paper fastener through the page.

5. Use the tab to hold and spin the circles to create a word with a beginning digraph sound and an ending sound. Write the word below the circle. Continue to spin the circles and find new words with the beginning digraph sounds. Write each word on the bottom of the page.

Reflect on Learning

To complete the left-hand page, have students draw four wheels with four spokes each. Then, students should write a beginning consonant digraph in the middle of each wheel. Instruct students to write different words that begin with each digraph on the spokes of the wheels.

Beginning Consonant Digraphs

A **beginning consonant diagraph** combines two consonant sounds at the beginning of a word to make a new sound.

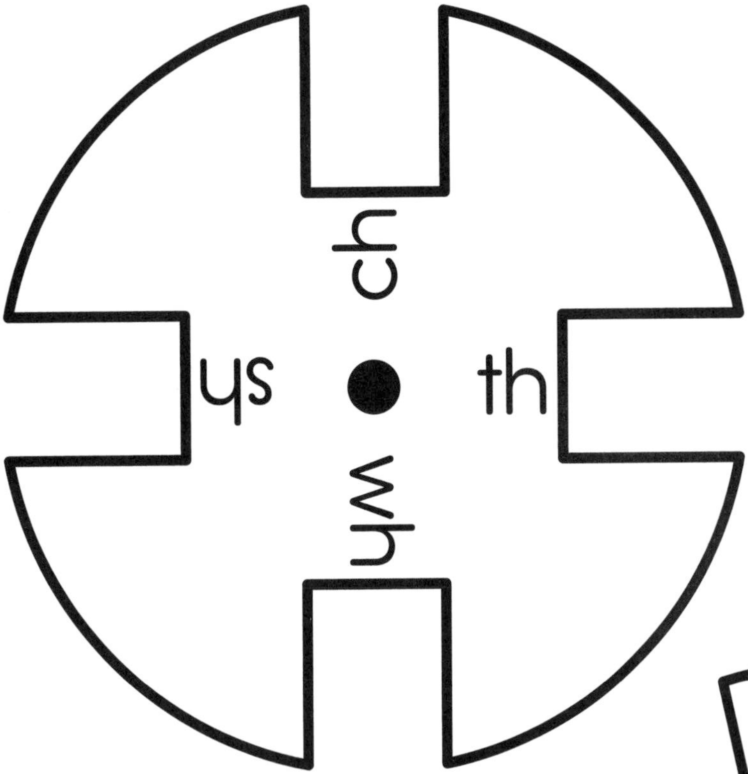

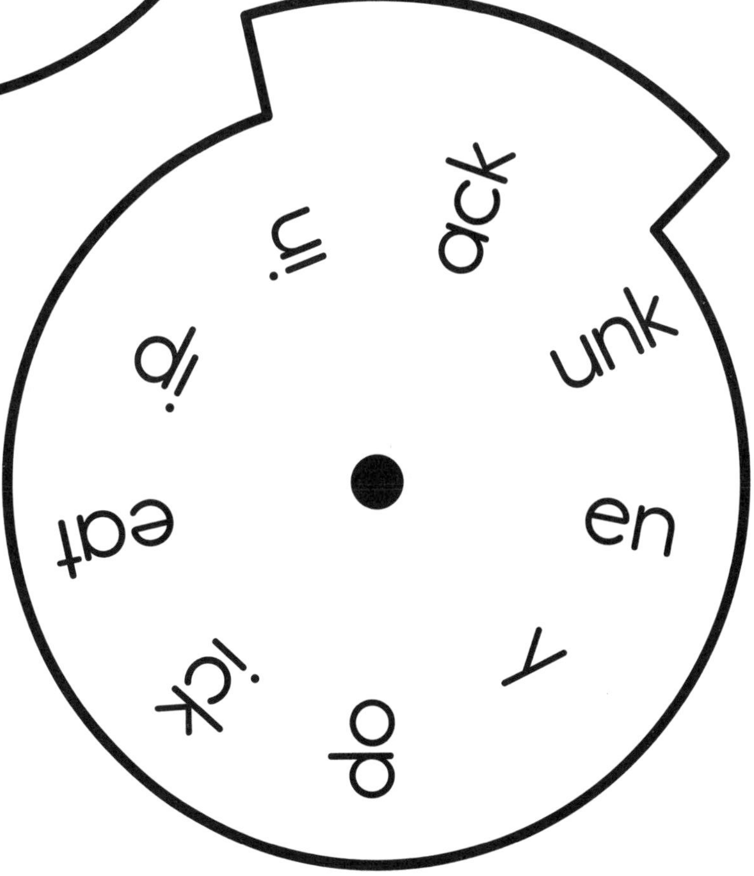

ch

sh · th

wh

ack

in

ip · unk

eat

en

ick

y

op

glue

Ending Consonant Digraphs

Students will need a sharpened pencil and a paper clip to complete the spinner activity.

Introduction

Write several -*ch*, -*sh*, and -*th* ending consonant digraph words on the board. Say the words aloud. Explain that a consonant digraph combines two consonant sounds to make a new sound. Discuss how the consonant digraph produces the new sound at the end in each word. Ask students to give more examples of words with ending consonant digraphs. Write them on the board as the students say them. Have volunteers come to the board and underline the ending consonant digraph in each word.

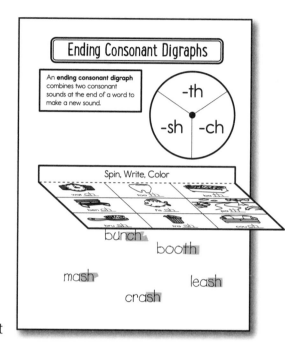

Creating the Notebook Page

Guide students through the following steps to complete the right-hand page in their notebooks.

1. Add a Table of Contents entry for the Ending Consonant Digraphs pages.

2. Cut out the title and glue it to the top of the page.

3. Cut out the definition piece and glue it to the left side of the page below the title. Discuss what an ending consonant digraph is.

4. Cut out the spinner and glue it beside the definition piece.

5. Cut out the flap. Apply glue to the back of the top section and attach it to the bottom of the page.

6. Use a sharpened pencil and a paper clip to create a spinner. Match each ending digraph spun to a picture on the flap. Fill in the blank with the ending digraph and color the picture. Continue spinning until each word on the flap is complete.

7. Brainstorm more words that contain the same ending consonant digraph sounds and write them under the flap. Highlight the consonant digraph in each word.

Reflect on Learning

To complete the left-hand page, have each student draw a tic-tac-toe board. With partners, students should take turns writing words with ending consonant digraphs in the boxes. The first student to get three correct words across, down, or diagonally wins the round. Have students play another round in their partners' notebooks.

Ending Consonant Digraphs

An **ending consonant digraph** combines two consonant sounds at the end of a word to make a new sound.

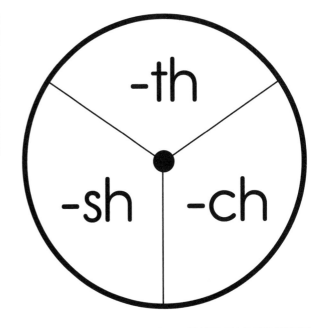

-th

-sh   -ch

Spin, Write, Color

wat _____	too _____	ba _____
ben _____	fi _____	pa _____
bru _____	tra _____	cou _____

Syllables

Introduction

Explain that a syllable is a unit of speech with one vowel sound. Write several one- and two-syllable words on the board. Have students listen as you identify and clap the number of syllables in each word. Then, have each student say her name aloud and clap the syllables. Have students clap out other words to hear how many syllables each word has.

Creating the Notebook Page

Guide students through the following steps to complete the right-hand page in their notebooks.

1. Add a Table of Contents entry for the Syllables pages.

2. Cut out the title and glue it to the top of the page.

3. Cut out the definition piece and glue it below the title. Complete the explanation. (Words are made up of parts called **syllables**.)

4. Cut out the two pockets. Apply glue to the back of the left and right sides and the bottom of each pocket and attach them side by side to the middle of the page.

5. Cut out the pencils. Say the word on each pencil and decide if it contains one or two syllables. Then, sort the words into the correct pockets.

6. Draw a T-chart below the pockets. Label the sides of the chart *one* and *two*. Write three more one- and two-syllable words in the correct columns.

Reflect on Learning

To complete the left-hand page, have students draw lines to divide their pages into two columns labeled *One Syllable* and *Two Syllables*. Write 10 one- and two-syllable words on the board. Then, have students write the words in the correct columns.

Syllables

Words are made up of parts called _____. Each **syllable** has a vowel sound. One way to count syllables is to clap as you say the word.

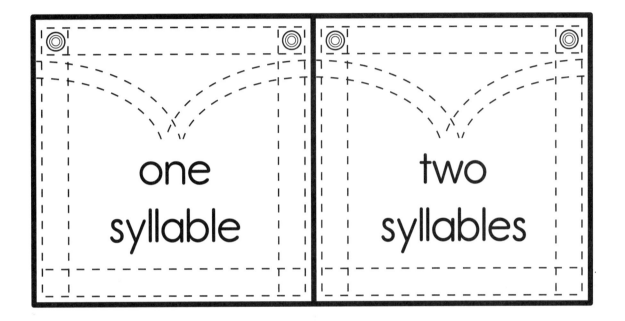

one syllable

two syllables

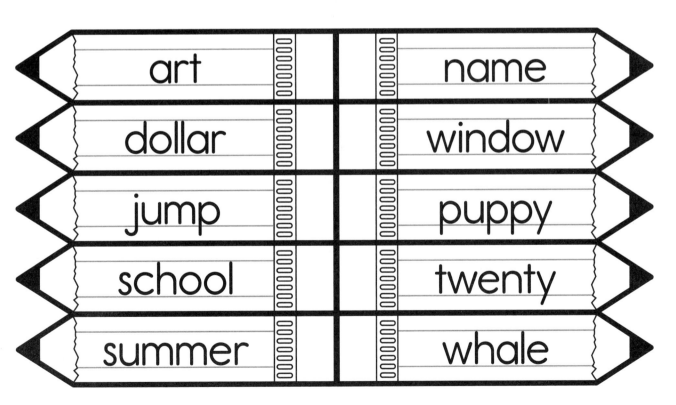

art

dollar

jump

school

summer

name

window

puppy

twenty

whale

Collective Nouns

Introduction

Define a collective noun as a noun that names one group of people, animals, or things. Display a picture of a flock of birds. Explain that one bird is a noun because it is a thing. Discuss how more than one bird is called a flock of birds and *flock* is the collective noun used to describe the birds. Then, have six volunteers stand together at the front of the room. Ask students to describe what they see. A possible answer may be that they see a group of students. As a class, identify the collective nouns used to describe the students. Have students brainstorm more collective nouns. Write them on the board as the students say them.

Creating the Notebook Page

Guide students through the following steps to complete the right-hand page in their notebooks.

1. Add a Table of Contents entry for the Collective Nouns pages.

2. Cut out the title and glue it to the top of the page.

3. Cut out the three flaps. Apply glue to the back of the top section of each flap and attach it to the page.

4. Cut out the collective noun cards. Fill in the blank on each card with a noun that makes it complete (for example, *A flock of **birds***).

5. Sort and glue the sentences under the flaps in the correct categories. (Answers will vary.) Highlight the collective noun in each sentence.

6. On the back of each flap, draw a picture to illustrate one of the collective nouns used under the flap.

Reflect on Learning

To complete the left-hand page, have students choose two of the collective nouns from the introduction and write sentences using each one. Then, have students draw pictures to illustrate each sentence.

Collective Nouns

People

Animals

Things

A crowd of ___ ___	A galaxy of ___ ___	A group of ___ ___
A flock of ___ ___	A swarm of ___ ___	A bunch of ___ ___

Irregular Plural Nouns

Introduction

Write regular nouns on index cards. Give one card to each student and have him write the plural form of his noun on the back of the index card. Allow students to share their plural nouns with partners. As a class, review the rules of pluralizing regular plural nouns. Explain that some nouns do not follow the rules. Write *The child played with the toy* on the board. Challenge students to make *child* plural and allow students to share their ideas.

Creating the Notebook Page

Guide students through the following steps to complete the right-hand page in their notebooks.

1. Add a Table of Contents entry for the Irregular Plural Nouns pages.

2. Cut out the title and glue it to the top of the page.

3. Cut out the flap book. Cut on the solid lines to create eight flaps. Apply glue to the back of the center section and attach it to the page.

4. On the back of each flap, write the regular form of the word for each picture shown.

5. Cut out the word cards. Sort and glue the cards under the correct flaps.

Reflect on Learning

To complete the left-hand page, have students write the following sentences in their notebooks: *As the _____ were talking, _____ started falling from the sky! Soon, _____ were everywhere, and it took the _____ forever to clean up.* Or, provide students with copies to glue in their notebooks. Have students write an irregular plural noun in each blank to complete a silly story.

Irregular Plural Nouns

Irregular plural **nouns** are nouns that do not follow the rules!

mice	leaves	feet	women
teeth	men	children	geese

Irregular Verbs

Introduction

Write three versions of a simple sentence where the verb tense changes, such as *Carson walked the dog, Carson walks the dog,* and *Carson will walk the dog.* Write enough sentences for each student to have one. Give each student one sentence. Have students read their sentences and move to different areas of the room, depending on if their sentences show past, present, or future tense. Have students share how they knew which tense their verbs were in. Then, discuss how irregular verbs use a different form of the same word to tell the past tense.

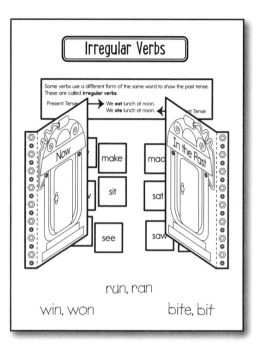

Creating the Notebook Page

Guide students through the following steps to complete the right-hand page in their notebooks.

1. Add a Table of Contents entry for the Irregular Verbs pages.

2. Cut out the title and glue it to the top of the page.

3. Cut out the *Some verbs use* piece and glue it below the title.

4. Cut out the time machine doors. Apply glue to the back of the narrow left or right side of each door. Attach the doors to the middle of the page, placing the pieces so that the inside edges of the doors align.

5. Cut out the word cards. Read each word and decide if it is used in the present tense or the past tense. Glue the word under the correct door.

6. Write more pairs of irregular verbs below the doors.

Reflect on Learning

To complete the left-hand page, have each student write a short story about a favorite field trip. Students should use at least five irregular verbs in their stories. Have students circle each irregular verb.

Irregular Verbs

Some verbs use a different form of the same word to show the past tense. These are called **irregular verbs**.

Present Tense ➤ We **eat** lunch at noon.

We **ate** lunch at noon. ◀ Past Tense

Now

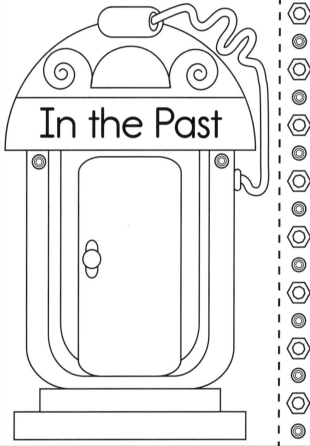

In the Past

sit	do	did	see	sat	made
say	said	know	make	knew	saw

Adjectives and Adverbs

Introduction

Gather and display a variety of balls of different sizes, shapes, colors, etc. Place an index card labeled with a letter near each ball. Have each student secretly choose one of the balls and take turns describing it to a partner. Each partner should guess the letter of the ball being described. As a class, discuss what kinds of words were helpful when students described the balls to their partners (adjectives).

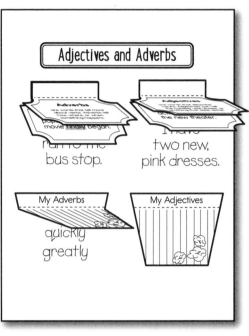

Creating the Notebook Page

Guide students through the following steps to complete the right-hand page in their notebooks.

1. Add a Table of Contents entry for the Adjectives and Adverbs pages.

2. Cut out the title and glue it to the top of the page.

3. Cut out the movie ticket flaps. Apply glue to the gray glue sections of the example flaps and place the definition flaps on top to create two two-flap books. Apply glue to the back of the top sections and attach the flap books to the page below the title.

4. For each flap, read and discuss the definition. Then, open the flap to the example flap. Read and highlight the adjectives or adverbs in each sentence. (*I have seen **three action** movies at the **new** theater. I **slowly** ate my popcorn as the movie **finally** began.*) Under the last flap, write a complete sentence using adjectives or adverbs.

5. Cut out the *My Adjectives* and *My Adverbs* flaps. Apply glue to the back of the top sections and attach them side by side on the bottom of the page.

6. As you find adjectives and adverbs in things you read, write them under the correct flaps. Use this page as a reference tool.

Reflect on Learning

To complete the left-hand page, have each student choose a ball from the introduction and write a description of it using several adjectives. Then, have students use adverbs to describe how the ball would move and bounce. Students should circle the adjectives and adverbs used in their descriptions.

Adjectives and Adverbs

Adjectives

are words that describe nouns. Adjectives can tell number, size, shape, or anything that adds detail.

I have seen three action movies at the new theater.

Adverbs

are words that tell more about verbs. Adverbs tell how, where, or when something happens.

I slowly ate my popcorn as the movie finally began.

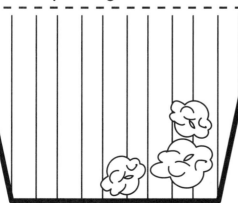

My Adjectives

My Adverbs

Writing a Sentence

Introduction

Write several sentences on the board that begin with lowercase letters and have no ending punctuation. Have students correct them. As a class, discuss what was wrong with each sentence and why.

Creating the Notebook Page

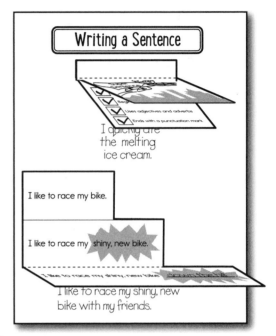

Guide students through the following steps to complete the right-hand page in their notebooks.

1. Add a Table of Contents entry for the Writing a Sentence pages.

2. Cut out the title and glue it to the top of the page.

3. Cut out the *Super Sentence* and checklist flaps. Apply glue to the gray glue section of the checklist flap and place the *Super Sentence* flap on top to create a two-flap book. Apply glue to the back of the top section and attach it to the page below the title.

4. Open the flap and read the checklist to review the elements of a complete sentence. Under the last flap, use the checklist to write a complete super sentence.

5. Cut out the stair-step sentence piece. Apply glue to the back of the top and middle sections and attach it to the bottom of the page.

6. Read the first two sentences. Compare the two sentences and discuss why using adjectives in the second sentence improves it by allowing the reader to visualize the bike. Read the second sentence aloud and replace *shiny, new bike* with another pair of adjectives and a noun. Then, fold the right edge of the last section in to the word *bike* to cover the blank line. Open the flap and write descriptive words to complete the super sentence.

7. Under the flap, write a new super sentence. Share your sentence with a partner.

Reflect on Learning

To complete the left-hand page, write a few simple incomplete sentences on the board, such as *the cat played* and *Dion was bored*. Have students improve the sentences by following the *Super Sentence* checklist on the right-hand page.

Writing a Sentence

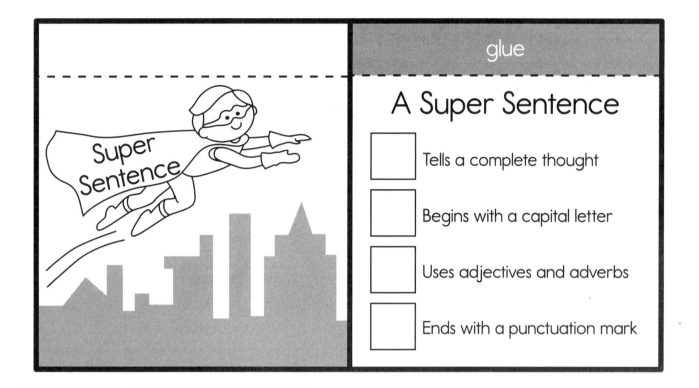

glue

A Super Sentence

☐ Tells a complete thought

☐ Begins with a capital letter

☐ Uses adjectives and adverbs

☐ Ends with a punctuation mark

I like to race my bike.

I like to race my shiny, new bike.

I like to race my shiny, new bike _____ .

Types of Sentences

Write three sentences on the board: *I made some popcorn. May I have some popcorn?* and *I love popcorn!* Discuss the subject of each sentence (popcorn) and who is saying each sentence (I). As a class, discuss why the sentences seem so different although the same person is talking about the same subject. Explain that there are different types of sentences, and each type serves a different purpose.

Creating the Notebook Page

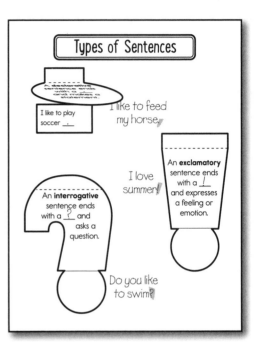

Guide students through the following steps to complete the right-hand page in their notebooks.

1. Add a Table of Contents entry for the Types of Sentences pages.

2. Cut out the title and glue it to the top of the page.

3. Cut out the punctuation flaps. Apply glue to the back of the top section of each one and attach it to the page.

4. Read each flap and discuss the different types of sentences. Then, fill in the correct punctuation mark for each type of sentence.

5. Cut out the sentence cards. Read each sentence. Then, fill in the correct punctuation mark. Glue each sentence card under the correct flap.

6. Write a declarative, interrogative, and exclamatory sentence beside each flap. Highlight the punctuation mark in each sentence.

Reflect on Learning

To complete the left-hand page, have each student choose a subject such as popcorn from the introductory lesson, or soccer from the right-hand page, and write three sentences about the subject. Each student should write one declarative sentence, one interrogative sentence, and one exclamatory sentence.

Types of Sentences

A **declarative** sentence ends with a ___ and makes a statement.

I like to play soccer ___

Our team won first place ___

Do you like to play soccer ___

An **interrogative** sentence ends with a ___ and asks a question.

An **exclamatory** sentence ends with a ___ and expresses a feeling or emotion.

Compound Words

Introduction

Define a compound word as two words put together to make a new word with a new meaning. Write the word *snow* on the board. Have a student tell you what it means. Write the word *man* below *snow.* Have a student read the word *man* and tell you what it means. Next, write the word *snowman* and ask if students notice anything about the new word. Discuss how the words *snow* and *man* are both in the new word. Circle each word in *snowman.* Explain that *snowman* is a compound word.

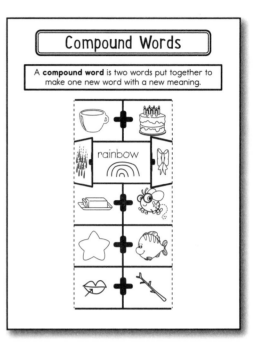

Creating the Notebook Page

Guide students through the following steps to complete the right-hand page in their notebooks.

1. Add a Table of Contents entry for the Compound Words pages.

2. Cut out the title and glue it to the top of the page.

3. Cut out the *A compound word is* piece and glue it below the title. Read and discuss what makes a compound word.

4. Cut out the flap book. Cut on the solid lines to create five flaps on each side. Place the piece facedown. For each pair of flaps, fold the two flaps in so that they align to create a plus sign. Apply glue to the gray glue section and attach it to the page.

5. Look at the picture on the left side. Then, look at the picture on the right side. Read the two words. Say the compound word that the two words make. Open the flaps and write the compound word under the two flaps. Then, draw a picture to illustrate the word.

6. Think of another compound word. On the last pair of flaps, draw a picture of the first word of the compound word on the left side. Draw a picture of the second word on the right side. Open the flaps and write the new word under the two flaps. Then, draw a picture to illustrate the word.

Reflect on Learning

To complete the left-hand page, have students brainstorm more compound words. Write the words on the board as the students say them. Have students copy the list into their notebooks. Next, each student should choose a word from the list, write a complete sentence with the word, and then draw a picture to illustrate the sentence.

Compound Words

A **compound word** is two words put together to make one new word with a new meaning.

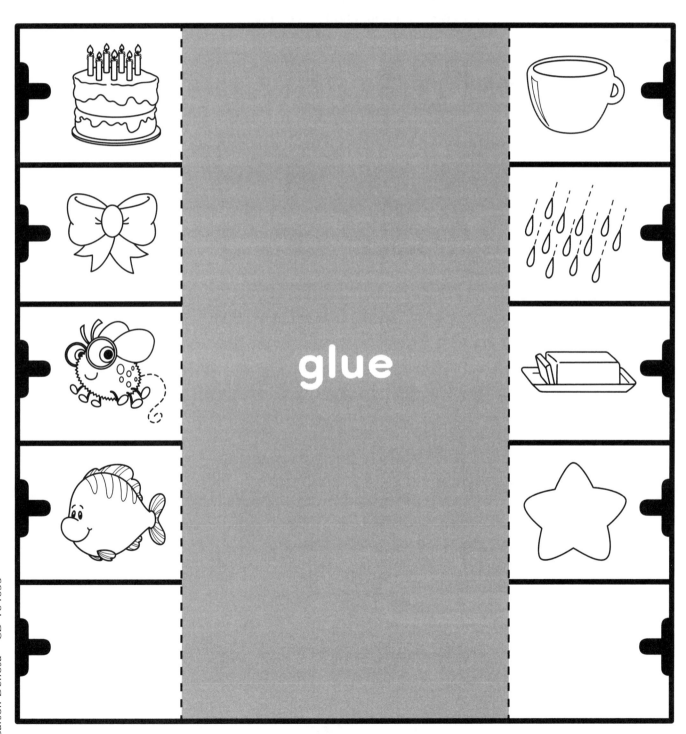

glue

Contractions

Introduction

Explain that a contraction is two words that are put together to make one word and that some of the letters drop out of the second word when the words are joined. Discuss how an apostrophe takes the place of the dropped letters. Divide the class into five teams. Give each team a book or magazine. Tell each team they will have five minutes to look for contractions and write them down. Allow time for each team to share their contractions.

Creating the Notebook Page

Guide students through the following steps to complete the right-hand page in their notebooks.

1. Add a Table of Contents entry for the Contractions pages.

2. Cut out the title and glue it to the top of the page.

3. Cut out the definition piece and glue it below the title

4. Complete the definition. (A **contraction** is two words that are put together to make one word.)

5. Cut out the contraction strips. For each strip, apply glue to the back of the left section and attach it to the left side of the page. Fold the right-hand side to the left to create a fold on the left-hand dashed line. Then, fold the top section back to the right to create a fold on the right-hand dashed line. When done, the contraction strip should have an accordion fold in it.

6. For each contraction strip, use the folds to practice reading the two words and the contraction that the two words make. Then, fill in the blank to complete the contraction.

Reflect on Learning

To complete the left-hand page, write *she is, they are, we will,* and *have not* on the board. Have students draw four large cupcakes with icing. Students should copy the pairs of words on the board on the bottom portion of their cupcakes. Then, have students write the contraction for each pair of words on the icing. Students should label the page *Cupcake Contractions.*

Contractions

A _____ is two words that are put together to make one word. Some of the letters drop out of the second word when the words are joined. An apostrophe takes the place of the dropped letters.

did + not = didn't

I am	_____	'm
do not	_____	n't
we are	_____	're
that is	_____	's
they will	_____	'll

Homophones

Introduction

Say the sentences *Last night I ate supper* and *A spider has eight legs*. Have students identify the two words that sound the same in the sentences. Write *ate* and *eight* on the board. Have students identify which word belongs in each sentence. Discuss how students knew which word you meant in each sentence. Explain that words that sound the same but have different meanings and often have different spellings are called *homophones*.

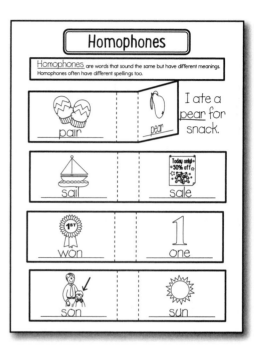

Creating the Notebook Page

Guide students through the following steps to complete the right-hand page in their notebooks.

1. Add a Table of Contents entry for the Homophones pages.

2. Cut out the title and glue it to the top of the page.

3. Cut out the definition and glue it below the title.

4. Complete the definition. (**Homophones** are words that sound the same but have different meanings.)

5. Cut out the four flap books. Apply glue to the back of the center section of each one and attach it to the page.

6. For each flap, look at the pictures. Decide on the correct spelling for the homophone each picture represents. Write the word on the flap. Under the flap, write a sentence with each word. Underline the homophone in each sentence.

Reflect on Learning

To complete the left-hand page, brainstorm as a class and write other homophone pairs on the board. Have students choose two pairs of homophones. Students should write two sentences for each pair, for a total of four sentences.

Homophones

_____ are words that sound the same but have different meanings. Homophones often have different spellings too.

_____	_____
_____	_____
_____	_____
_____	_____

Prefixes

Introduction

Write several words with prefixes, such as *preheat*, *pregame*, *rewind*, *review*, *unafraid*, and *unclear* on the board. Have students identify familiar parts of the words, or base words, by underlining them (such as *heat* in *preheat*). Explain that each of the words on the board has a prefix added to it, which changes the meaning.

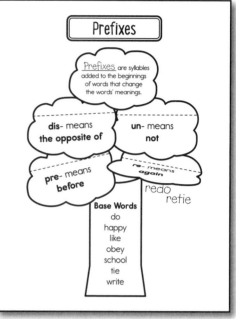

Creating the Notebook Page

Guide students through the following steps to complete the right-hand page in their notebooks.

1. Add a Table of Contents entry for the Prefixes pages.

2. Cut out the title and glue it to the top of the page.

3. Cut out the *Base Words* piece and glue it near the bottom of the page.

4. Cut out each flap. Apply glue to the back of the top section of each flap and attach it to the page to create a tree.

5. Cut out the definition piece and glue it to the top of the tree.

6. Complete the definition. (**Prefixes** are syllables added to the beginnings of words that change the words' meanings.)

7. On each flap, read the definition of each prefix. Then, look at the base words. Use the base words to create two words with each prefix. Write the words under the flaps. Discuss the meanings of the words under each flap with a partner.

Reflect on Learning

To complete the left-hand page, have students use each word under the flaps on the right-hand side to write a complete sentence. Then, have them underline the prefix in each word.

Prefixes

_____ are syllables added to the beginnings of words that change the words' meanings.

pre- means **before**

re- means **again**

un- means **not**

dis- means **the opposite of**

Base Words
do
happy
like
obey
school
tie
write

Suffixes

Students will need a brass paper fastener to complete this page.

Introduction

Write several verbs on the board, such as *jump, laugh,* and *yell.* Then, add -*ed* to each word. As a class, discuss how the meaning of each word changed (it became past tense). Repeat with nouns such as *balloon, orange,* and *shoe,* and the suffix -*s.* Explain that -*ed* and -*s* are common suffixes that are added to the ends of words to change their meanings.

Creating the Notebook Page

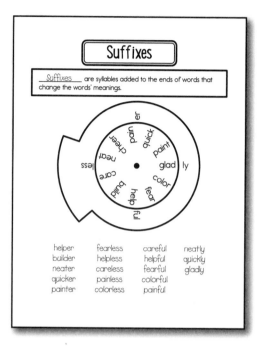

Guide students through the following steps to complete the right-hand page in their notebooks.

1. Add a Table of Contents entry for the Suffixes pages.

2. Cut out the title and glue it to the top of the page.

3. Cut out the definition piece and glue it below the title.

4. Complete the definition. (**Suffixes** are syllables added to the ends of words that change the words' meanings.)

5. Cut out the three circles. Place the words circle on top of the suffixes circle and then place the smallest circle on the bottom with the gray side down. Push a brass paper fastener through the dot at the center to connect the circles. (It may be helpful to create the hole in each piece separately first.) Apply glue to the gray glue section and attach it below the definition piece. Both circles should spin freely. Do not press the brass paper fastener through the page.

6. Use the tab to hold and spin the wheels to create a word with a base word and a suffix. Write the word on the page below the circle. Continue to spin the circles and find new words. Write the words as you find them.

Reflect on Learning

To complete the left-hand page, have students use the words they wrote on the right-hand page to write at least four sentences. Students should underline each suffix used in the sentences.

Suffixes

_____ are syllables added to the ends of words that change the words' meanings.

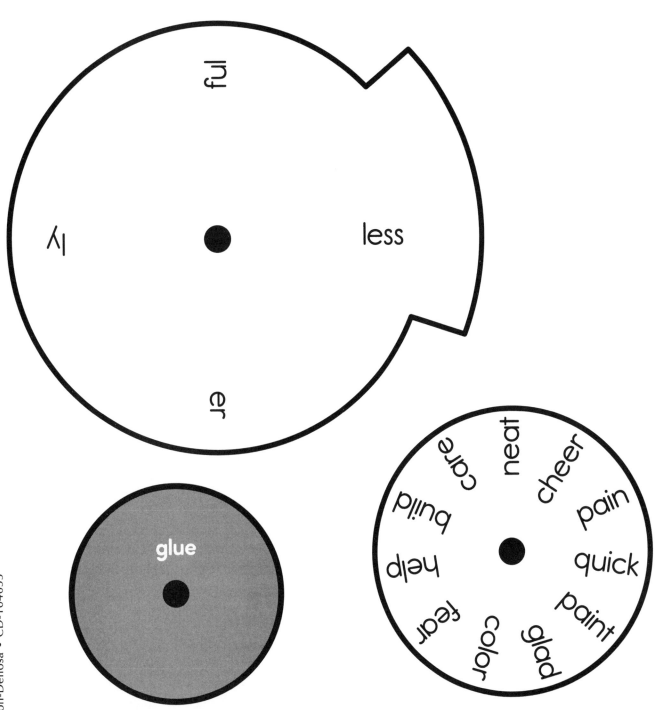

Synonyms

Introduction

Have students stand behind their desks. Say several related verbs for students to act out, such as *stretch, grow,* and *reach; crouch, duck,* and *dodge,* or *jump, hop,* and *bounce.* As a class, discuss how the actions students completed were similar, and why. Then, discuss how the verbs were similar, but not exactly the same. Introduce that synonyms often mean the same thing, but they can be slightly different in meaning.

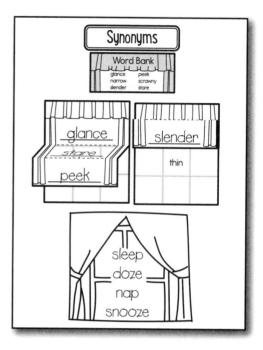

Creating the Notebook Page

Guide students through the following steps to complete the right-hand page in their notebooks.

1. Add a Table of Contents entry for the Synonyms pages.

2. Cut out the title and glue it to the top of the page.

3. Cut out the word bank and glue it below the title.

4. Cut out the curtain flaps. For each flap, fold on the dashed lines, alternating the fold direction. Set aside.

5. Cut out the window flaps. Apply glue to the gray glue sections and place a curtain flap on top to create a two-flap book. Then, glue the window pieces to the page below the word bank.

6. Read the word on each window. Then, use the word bank to find three synonyms for each word. Write the words on each curtain flap. Fold each curtain up and down to read the synonyms for the word on the window.

7. Finally, draw a window on the bottom of the page and write the word *sleep* near the top of the window. Then, write two or more synonyms for the word *sleep.*

Reflect on Learning

To complete the left-hand page, have students choose a set of three synonyms such as the examples on the right-hand page, the verbs from the introduction, or a set of their choosing. Students should use each word in a separate sentence. Sentences should show the slight differences in meanings between the synonyms.

Synonyms

Word Bank

glance   peek

narrow   scrawny

slender   stare

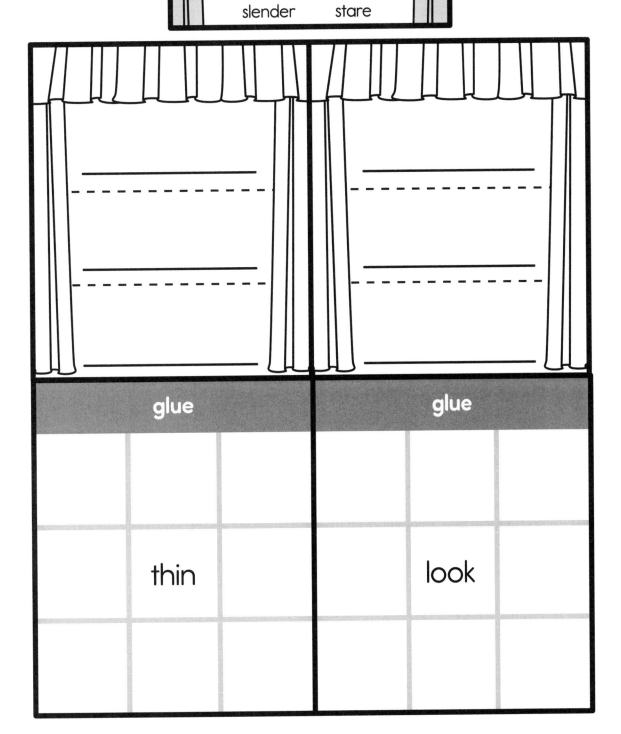

glue

glue

thin

look

Using Commas

Introduction

Review commas used in dates and items in a series. Provide each student with a self-stick note. Have each student draw a comma on his self-stick note. On the board, write several dates and sentences that contain lists. Leave the commas out of each sentence. Have students place their self-stick notes on the board to add commas to the correct places in the dates and sentences.

Creating the Notebook Page

Guide students through the following steps to complete the right-hand page in their notebooks.

1. Add a Table of Contents entry for the Using Commas pages.

2. Cut out the title and glue it to the top of the page.

3. Cut out the written letter piece and glue it below the title. Read the letter and highlight the commas used.

4. Cut out the envelope piece. Apply glue to the back of the left and right sides and the bottom of the envelope and attach it below the written letter to create a pocket.

5. Cut out the blank letter piece. Write a letter to a friend. Be sure to use commas in the correct places. Place the completed letter into the envelope.

6. Address the envelope to your friend. Be sure to use commas in the correct places.

Reflect on Learning

To complete the left-hand page, have each student draw a rectangle to resemble an envelope and "address" the envelope to a friend or family member. Then, each student should write a letter to that person, using correct punctuation throughout.

Using Commas

June 24, 2015

Hi Seth,
    I am having so much fun at summer camp. I swam in a lake, went horseback riding, and sang songs around a campfire. I wish you had been able to come. I'll be home next week. See you soon!
                                    Later,

                                    Ryan

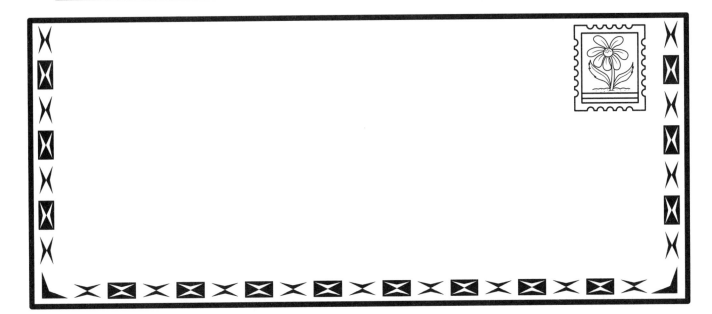

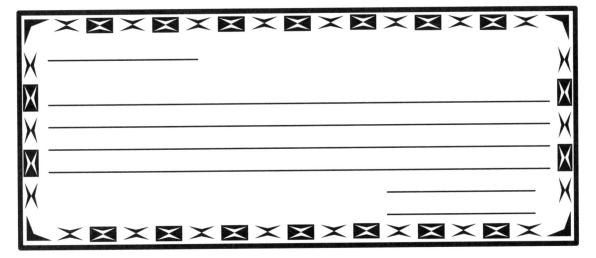

Fiction and Nonfiction

Introduction

Display several books the class has recently read. Briefly discuss each book, including the topic, characters (if any), setting (if any), etc. Ask students to identify which books had facts and which books were make-believe. Have students sort the books into two categories based on that criteria. Introduce the terms *fiction* and *nonfiction*.

Creating the Notebook Page

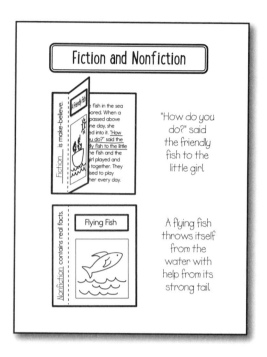

Guide students through the following steps to complete the right-hand page in their notebooks.

1. Add a Table of Contents entry for the Fiction and Nonfiction pages.

2. Cut out the title and glue it to the top of the page.

3. Cut out the cover flaps. Complete the definition on each book. (**Fiction** is make-believe. **Nonfiction** contains real facts.)

4. Cut out the two story flaps. Read each story and decide if it is fiction or nonfiction. Then, apply glue to the gray glue sections and place the correct cover flaps on top to create two two-flap books. Then, glue the flap books to the page.

5. Cut out the story titles. Read the stories and decide which title belongs to each story. Apply glue to the gray glue sections on top of the flaps and attach each title to the correct flap. Then, draw a cover illustration for each book.

6. Beside each book, write one sentence from the story that helped you decide if the story was fiction or nonfiction.

Reflect on Learning

To complete the left-hand page, show the class two or more books. Describe each book, including the title, cover, and interior pages. Share a few pages and some text from each. Students should write the title of each book and whether it is a fiction or nonfiction book.

Fiction and Nonfiction

| Flying Fish | A Friendly Fish |

_____ is make-believe.

glue

glue

Flying fish do not fly like birds do. A flying fish throws itself from the water with help from its strong tail. Once it is in the air, it spreads its large fins. The fins act like the wings of a glider.

_____ contains real facts.

glue

glue

A little fish in the sea was bored. When a boat passed above her one day, she jumped into it. "How do you do?" said the friendly fish to the little girl. The fish and the little girl played and swam together. They promised to play together every day.

Author's Purpose

Introduction

Before the lesson, gather several sets of instructions from board or card games, several fiction picture books, and several brochures for local attractions. Divide students into small groups. Provide each group with a set of instructions, a book, and a brochure. Have groups decide why they would read each text. Allow groups to share their ideas with the class. Then, discuss each group's reasoning.

I read <u>The Three Little Pigs</u>. The author's purpose was to entertain.

Creating the Notebook Page

Guide students through the following steps to complete the right-hand page in their notebooks.

1. Add a Table of Contents entry for the Author's Purpose pages.

2. Cut out the title and glue it to the top of the page.

3. Cut out the pie piece. Cut on the solid lines to create three flaps. Apply glue to the back of the center section and attach it below the title.

4. Cut out the fruit pieces. Read each piece. Match the definition to the author's purpose and glue it under the correct flap.

5. Cut out the title pieces. Decide which title best matches each author's purpose. Glue each title on the correct section of the pie.

6. Read a book of your choice. Then, write the title and the author's purpose for writing the book below the pie.

Reflect on Learning

To complete the left-hand page, have students draw lines to divide their pages into three columns labeled *Persuade*, *Inform*, and *Entertain*. As a class, brainstorm several different types of texts that fit in each category and write them on the board. For example, under *Inform*, students could write *recipes*, *instructions*, and *encyclopedias*.

Author's Purpose

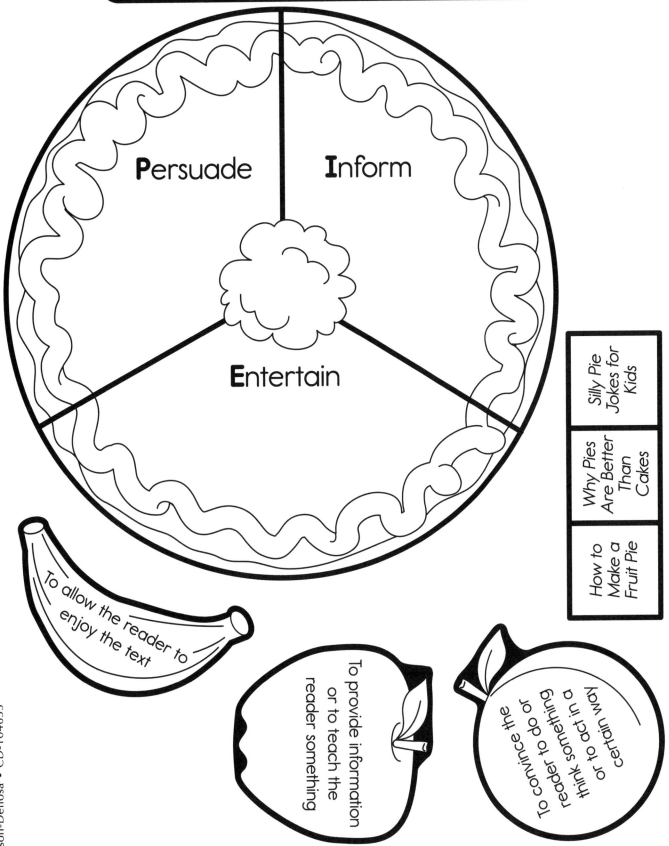

Persuade | Inform

Entertain

Silly Pie Jokes for Kids

Why Pies Are Better Than Cakes

How to Make a Fruit Pie

To allow the reader to enjoy the text

To provide information or to teach the reader something

To convince the reader to do or think something or to act in a certain way

Making Connections

Introduction

Tell a short story about something that students can relate to, such as going to a baseball game or watching a movie. Then, allow students to make connections and share similar stories. Discuss how students often are able to connect to stories because they have had something similar happen in their lives, or because they have heard about something that happened somewhere else in the world. Explain that good readers look for connections when they are reading as well.

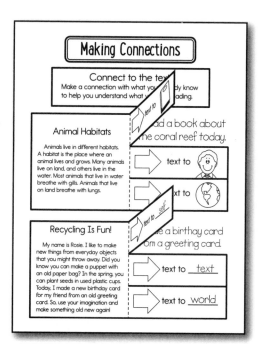

Creating the Notebook Page

Guide students through the following steps to complete the right-hand page in their notebooks.

1. Add a Table of Contents entry for the Making Connections pages.

2. Cut out the title and glue it to the top of the page.

3. Cut out the *Connect to the text!* piece and glue it below the title.

4. Discuss the different ways a reader can connect to a text.

5. Cut out the flap books. For each flap book, cut on the solid lines to create three flaps. Apply glue to the back of the left section and attach it to the page.

6. For the *Animal Habitats* story, read the story and make a connection to a book or movie you have read or seen before, a connection to a personal experience, and a connection to something you may know about animals around the world and where they live.

7. For the *Recycling Is Fun!* story, read the story and make a connection to the text under each flap. Fill in the blank on each flap to tell which type of connection you made (text to text, text to self, or text to world).

Reflect on Learning

To complete the left-hand page, have each student write about a connection he has with a recently read text. Each student should explain the connection and describe which of the three types of connection it is.

Making Connections

Animal Habitats

Animals live in different habitats. A habitat is the place where an animal lives and grows. Many animals live on land, and others live in the water. Most animals that live in water breathe with gills. Animals that live on land breathe with lungs.

text to

text to

text to

Recycling Is Fun!

My name is Rosie. I like to make new things from everyday objects that you might throw away. Did you know you can make a puppet with an old paper bag? In the spring, you can plant seeds in used plastic cups. Today, I made a new birthday card for my friend from an old greeting card. So, use your imagination and make something old new again!

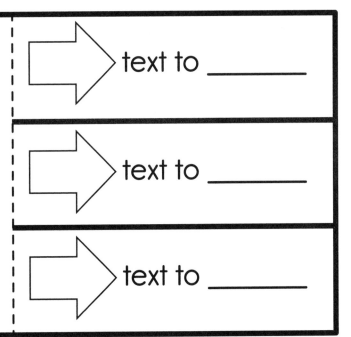

text to _____

text to _____

text to _____

Context Clues

Introduction

Read a wordless picture book with the class. Together, infer what is happening in the book. Discuss how you were able to use clues in the illustrations to figure out, or infer, what was happening. Explain that good readers can do the same thing with unknown words. They can use clues in the words and sentences around an unknown word to figure out its meaning.

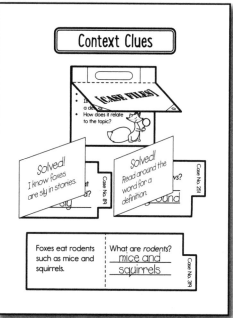

Creating the Notebook Page

Guide students through the following steps to complete the right-hand page in their notebooks.

1. Add a Table of Contents entry for the Context Clues pages.

2. Cut out the title and glue it to the top of the page.

3. Cut out the *Case Files* and *Clues to an unknown word* pieces. Apply glue to the gray glue section and place the *Case Files* piece on top of it to create a two-flap book. Glue the flap book below the title.

4. Cut out the case file folders. Apply glue to the back of the right-hand sections and attach them to the page. Fold on the dashed lines to close the folders. For each piece, read the case on the left side. Then, use context clues to fill in the blanks on the right side and solve the case.

5. On the front of each flap, write *Solved!* and which context clue you used to solve the case.

Reflect on Learning

To complete the left-hand page, write a sentence or paragraph on the board with an unfamiliar word in it. For example, *My brother likes to **krig** books. He can even **krig** chapter books! He likes to **krig** his books at recess.* Or, provide students with copies to glue in their notebooks. Have students write short definitions of the unfamiliar word and explain how they used context clues to figure it out.

Context Clues

glue

Clues to an unknown word:
- How is it used in the sentence?
- Is there an explanation or a definition?
- How does it relate to the topic?

Foxes often live in burrows, or holes in the ground.

What are *burrows*?

_____

_____

Case No. 251

The gingerbread man was tricked by the **ysl** fox!

The bold letters got mixed up. What is the correct word?

_____

Case No. 89

Foxes eat rodents such as mice and squirrels.

What are *rodents*?

_____

_____

Case No. 319

Story Structure

Introduction

Before the lesson, use paper clips to clip the beginning, middle, and end pages of a picture book together. Read the picture book to the class. But, read the sections out of order. As a class, discuss why the story was confusing. Explain that stories are generally organized into a beginning, middle, and end that have the same characteristics because it makes sense to the reader.

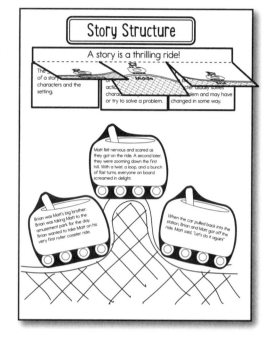

Creating the Notebook Page

Guide students through the following steps to complete the right-hand page in their notebooks.

1. Add a Table of Contents entry for the Story Structure pages.

2. Cut out the title and glue it to the top of the page.

3. Cut out the flap book. Cut on the solid lines to create three flaps. Apply glue to the back of the top section and attach it to the page below the title.

4. Cut out the definition pieces. For each piece, read and complete the definition of each story structure element. (The **beginning** of a story introduces the characters and the setting. The **middle** of a story is where the action takes place. At the **end** of a story, the main character usually solves the problem and may have changed in some way.) Then, glue the definition under the correct flap.

5. Cut out the roller coaster car pieces. Read each one and decide which car contains the beginning, middle, and end of the story. Draw a roller coaster track on the bottom of your page. Glue the cars on the track in the correct sequence. Read the story to make sure the story structure is correct.

Reflect on Learning

To complete the left-hand page, write the following questions on the board about the story from the bottom of the right-hand page and have students answer them: *Who are the characters in the story? Where is the setting? What is the problem in the story? How did Matt change from the beginning of the story to the end of the story?*

Story Structure

A story is a thrilling ride!

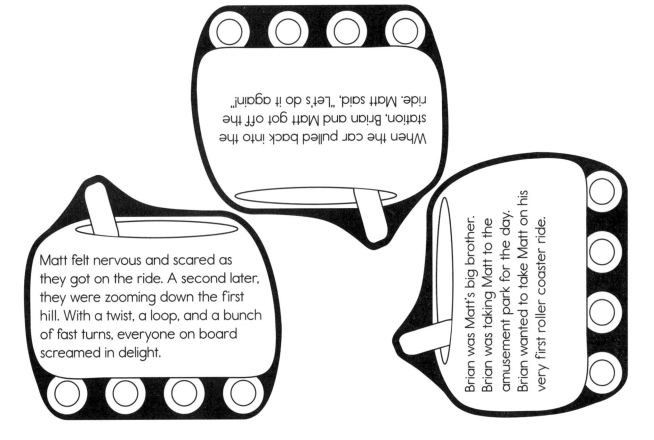

Beginning

Middle

End

The _____ of a story introduces the characters and the setting.	At the _____ of a story, the main character usually solves the problem and may have changed in some way.	The _____ of a story is where the action takes place. The character may react to or try to solve a problem.

When the car pulled back into the station, Brian and Matt got off the ride. Matt said, "Let's do it again!"

Matt felt nervous and scared as they got on the ride. A second later, they were zooming down the first hill. With a twist, a loop, and a bunch of fast turns, everyone on board screamed in delight.

Brian was Matt's big brother. Brian was taking Matt to the amusement park for the day. Brian wanted to take Matt on his very first roller coaster ride.

Key Details in a Story

Introduction

Explain that when journalists write articles, they often try to answer the five Ws (who, what, when, where, and why). Display a newspaper or magazine article and challenge students to find the answer to each W in the article. Discuss the details that provide the information. Explain that as in nonfiction writing, fiction stories include details that give the reader similar information.

Creating the Notebook Page

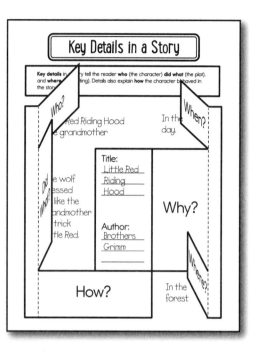

Guide students through the following steps to complete the right-hand page in their notebooks.

1. Add a Table of Contents entry for the Key Details in a Story pages.

2. Cut out the title and glue it to the top of the page.

3. Cut out the *Key details in a story* piece and glue it below the title.

4. Discuss what key details are and what information details can add to a story.

5. Cut out the questions piece. Cut on the solid lines to create two separate flap books with three flaps each and a separate *Title/Author* piece. Glue the *Title/Author* piece to the center of the page. Apply glue to the back of the left and right sections of the flap books and attach them to the page so that they surround the *Title/Author* piece.

6. Choose a book you have recently read. Write the title and author on the *Title/Author* piece. Under each flap, answer the question using key details from the book.

Reflect on Learning

To complete the left-hand page, have students imagine an author left one of the details from the right-hand page out of a story, such as *who* or *where*. Students should describe how it would affect the story and the reader.

Key Details in a Story

Key details in a story tell the reader **who** (the character) **did what** (the plot), and **where** (the setting). Details also explain **how** the character behaved in the story and **why**.

Who?	When?
Did What?	Title: _____ _____ _____ Author: _____ _____ _____	Why?
How?	Where?

Story Elements: Character

Introduction

Divide students into small groups and give each group a picture book. Have groups read their picture books and answer the question *Who?* Each group should create a small poster titled *Who is in _____?* and fill in the blank with the title of their group's book. Then, students should write and draw the answer to the question on the posters. Allow groups to share their posters with the class.

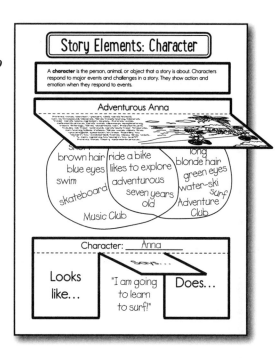

Creating the Notebook Page

Guide students through the following steps to complete the right-hand page in their notebooks.

1. Add a Table of Contents entry for the Story Elements: Character pages.

2. Cut out the title and glue it to the top of the page.

3. Cut out the *A character is* piece and glue it below the title.

4. Discuss what a character is and the role characters play in a story.

5. Cut out the *Adventurous Anna* flap. Apply glue to the back of the top section and attach it below the *A character is* piece.

6. Read the passage. Under the flap, draw a Venn diagram to compare yourself to Anna.

7. Cut out the *Character* flap. Cut on the solid lines to create three flaps. Apply glue to the back of the top section and attach it to the bottom of the page.

8. Using the *Adventurous Anna* passage above, complete the flap book. Fill in the character name. Under each flap, describe what the character looks like, says, and does.

Reflect on Learning

To complete the left-hand page, have each student list the characters from a recently read story. Then, each student should choose a character and complete the sentence stems from the right-hand page for that character.

60

Story Elements: Character

A **character** is the person, animal, or object that a story is about. Characters respond to major events and challenges in a story. They show action and emotion when they respond to events.

Adventurous Anna

Anna was seven years old and lived on a tropical island. She had long, blond hair and green eyes. Anna was adventurous and was always exploring new things. She started an Adventure Club at her school and led her friends on long bike rides. She was also the youngest person in her family to learn to water-ski! One day she said, "I am going to learn to surf!" Anna was very adventurous.

Character: _____

Looks like …	Says …	Does …

Story Elements: Setting

Introduction

Remind students of a story the class recently read. Have students discuss with partners how the story would have been different if it had taken place in the desert, in a snowstorm, at night, in outer space, or in the future. As a class, discuss how the setting, or where and when a story takes place, is an important part of the story.

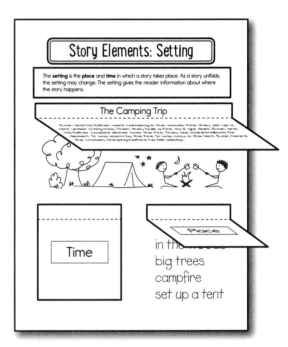

Creating the Notebook Page

Guide students through the following steps to complete the right-hand page in their notebooks.

1. Add a Table of Contents entry for the Story Elements: Setting pages.

2. Cut out the title and glue it to the top of the page.

3. Cut out *The setting is* flap. Apply glue to the back of the top section and attach it below the title. Discuss how the setting helps you understand a story.

4. Cut out *The Camping Trip* flap. Apply glue to the back of the top section and attach it to the page below *The setting is* flap. Read the story. Then, use details from the story to draw the setting under the flap.

5. Cut out the *Time* and *Place* flaps. Apply glue to the back of the top section of each flap and attach it near the bottom of the page. Under each flap, write words from the story that gave you clues to the time and place of the story.

Reflect on Learning

To complete the left-hand page, have each student identify the setting from a recently read story. Students should include the time and place in their descriptions.

62

Story Elements: Setting

The **setting** is the **place** and **time** in which a story takes place. As a story unfolds, the setting may change. The setting gives the reader information about where the story happens.

The Camping Trip

Evan and his father went camping in the woods. First, they set up a tent under a big tree. Then, they built a fire. As it got dark, Evan and his father cooked dinner over the fire. They ate marshmallows for dessert. It was warm by the fire. It was cozy in the tent. Evan heard the crickets chirping before he fell asleep.

Time

Place

Story Elements: Problem and Solution

Introduction

Tell students the beginnings of two short stories: *Once, there was a king who had a peaceful kingdom. He ruled fairly, and everyone in the land liked him. The people had plenty to eat and were happy* and *Once, there was a kind king. He was fair, but recently a dragon had started haunting his land. The king did not want to hurt the dragon, but he needed to find a way to keep his kingdom safe.* As a class, discuss the differences between the stories. Which is more interesting? Which story would you like to keep reading? Why? Explain that stories often have problems to allow the characters to do interesting things that keeps the reader's attention.

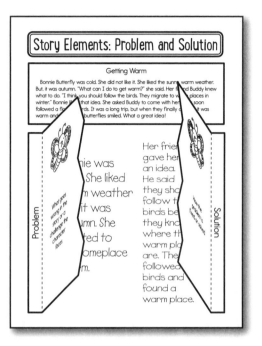

Creating the Notebook Page

Guide students through the following steps to complete the right-hand page in their notebooks.

1. Add a Table of Contents entry for the Story Elements: Problem and Solution pages.

2. Cut out the title and glue it to the top of the page.

3. Cut out the *Getting Warm* piece and glue it below the title.

4. Cut out the *Problem* and *Solution* piece. Cut on the solid line to create two flaps. Apply glue to the back of the left and right sections and attach them to the page so that the edges meet in the middle.

5. Read the passage. Under the *Problem* flap, write the problem from the passage. Under the *Solution* flap, write the solution from the passage.

Reflect on Learning

To complete the left-hand page, have each student identify a problem from a recently read story. Students should include the problem and how the problem was solved in their descriptions.

© Carson-Dellosa • CD-104653

Story Elements: Problem and Solution

Getting Warm

Bonnie Butterfly was cold. She did not like it. She liked the sunny, warm weather. But, it was autumn. "What can I do to get warm?" she said. Her friend Buddy knew what to do. "I think you should follow the birds. They migrate to warm places in winter." Bonnie liked that idea. She asked Buddy to come with her. They soon followed a flock of birds. It was a long trip, but when they finally arrived, it was warm and sunny! The butterflies smiled. What a great idea!

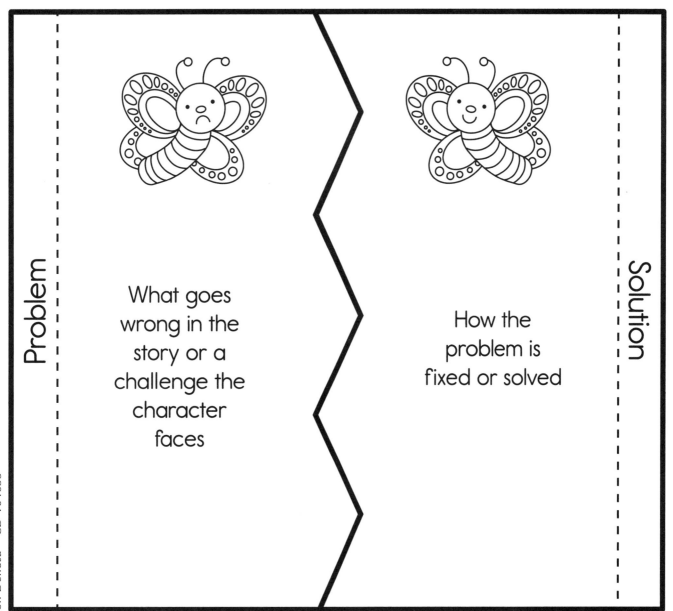

Problem

What goes wrong in the story or a challenge the character faces

Solution

How the problem is fixed or solved

Fables, Folktales, and Fairy Tales

This lesson can be taught over several days.

Introduction

Make a three-column chart on the board. Label the columns *fable*, *folktale*, and *fairy tale*. Discuss the differences between the three, listing common characteristics of each genre and predictable keywords such as *Once upon a time* (fairy tale), *tall tale* (folktale), or *moral of the story* (fable). Then, read aloud an example of each and ask students to decide which of the three it is. Add more keywords to the chart.

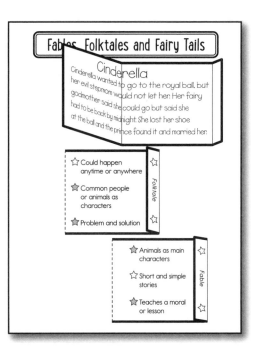

Creating the Notebook Page

Guide students through the following steps to complete the right-hand page in their notebooks.

1. Add a Table of Contents entry for the Fables, Folktales, and Fairy Tales pages.

2. Cut out the title and glue it to the top of the page.

3. Cut out the trifolds. Fold on the dashed lines to create each trifold. Apply glue to the back of the center section of each trifold and attach it to the page.

4. For each trifold, read a fable, a folktale, or a fairy tale. As you read each story, color the star on the front of the flap when you come across that story element. Then, open the flap and write a short summary of the book that describes at least one story element from the front of the flap.

Reflect on Learning

To complete the left-hand page, have students choose one of the genres from the right-hand page. Each student should design a poster and title it *Wanted: A Good _____ (Fable, Folktale, or Fairy Tale)*. The poster should include an illustration of a cover of a book from the chosen genre and characteristics of the genre. Allow time for students to share their work.

Fables, Folktales, and Fairy Tales

Fairy Tale

glue

☆ Type of folktale

☆ Magic elements

☆ Good vs. evil

Folktale

glue

☆ Could happen anytime or anywhere

☆ Common people or animals as characters

☆ Problem and solution

Fable

glue

☆ Animals as main characters

☆ Short and simple stories

☆ Teaches a moral or lesson

Poetry

Introduction

Recite the poem "Hickory Dickory Dock" as a class. Ask students how they know this is a poem. Discuss and identify rhyming words in the poem. Write *rhyme* on the board. Then, read "The Muffin Man." Make sure students notice the repetition in "The Muffin Man." Write *repetition* on the board. Finally, recite "Peter Piper" slowly. Then, try it again quickly. Encourage students to try to say the first line quickly. Write *alliteration* on the board and discuss that alliteration is repeating the first consonant sound in several words. Explain that these are three elements that writers use to write poetry.

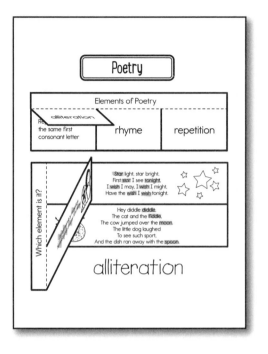

Creating the Notebook Page

Guide students through the following steps to complete the right-hand page in their notebooks.

1. Add a Table of Contents entry for the Poetry pages.

2. Cut out the title and glue it to the top of the page.

3. Cut out the *Elements of Poetry* flap book. Cut on the solid lines to create three flaps. Then, cut out the definition piece. Apply glue to the gray glue section and place the *Elements of Poetry* flap book on top to create a stacked six-flap book. Then, apply glue to the entire back of the definition piece and attach it to the page below the title.

4. Read each definition and discuss the different elements of poetry.

5. Cut out the *Which element is it?* flap book. Cut on the solid lines to create three flaps. Apply glue to the back of the left section and attach it to the page.

6. For each flap, read the poem. Then, decide which element the poem uses and write it under the flap. Highlight the words in the poem that helped you decide which element the poem uses.

Reflect on Learning

To complete the left-hand page, have students make acrostic poems by writing their own names vertically in capital letters. Then, students should use alliteration, rhyme, or repetition to complete poems about themselves. Allow time for students to share their work.

Poetry

Elements of Poetry

alliteration	rhyme	repetition
glue		
Repeated sounds of the same first consonant letter	Words with similar ending sounds	Repeated lines or words throughout the poem

Which element is it?

Star light, star bright,
First star I see tonight,
I wish I may, I wish I might,
Have the wish I wish tonight.

Hey diddle diddle,
The cat and the fiddle.
The cow jumped over the moon.
The little dog laughed
To see such sport,
And the dish ran away with the spoon.

Sally sells seashells by the seashore.
The shells Sally sells are surely from the sea.

Text Features

Introduction

Write *heading*, *table of contents*, *glossary*, *diagram*, *illustration*, and *map* on the board. Explain what each term means and show examples. Discuss how these features help readers find information quickly. Then, tell students they will go on a scavenger hunt. Give students various magazines and books that contain pages with examples of each text feature. Have students work in teams of four, each with a different magazine and book. Ask teams to quietly stand once they think they have found all six text features.

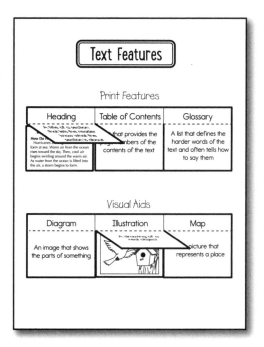

Creating the Notebook Page

Guide students through the following steps to complete the right-hand page in their notebooks.

1. Add a Table of Contents entry for the Text Features pages.

2. Cut out the title and glue it to the top of the page.

3. Cut out each flap book. Cut on the solid lines to create three flaps on each one. Apply glue to the back of the top section of each flap book and attach it to the page. Decide which flap book describes print features and which one describes visual aids. Label the flap books.

4. Cut out the text features example cards. Look at each card. Decide which text feature is shown on the card. Glue the card under the correct flap.

Reflect on Learning

To complete the left-hand page, have students choose one text feature shown on the right-hand page. Students should write the text feature and describe the importance of it to readers.

Text Features

Heading	Table of Contents	Glossary
A title of a section that lets the reader know what the section is about	A list that provides the page numbers of the contents of the text	A list that defines the harder words of the text and often tells how to say them

Diagram	Illustration	Map
An image that shows the parts of something	A drawing of a real object	A picture that represents a place

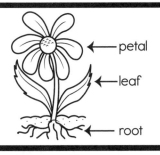

asteroid *(AS-tur-oyd)*: a small rocky body that orbits the sun

atmosphere *(AT-muss-feer)*: the area surrounding a planet that is filled with gas

comet *(KOM-it)*: a body that orbits the sun and has a bright tail

Hurricanes
How Do Hurricanes Form?
  Hurricanes are huge storms that form at sea. Warm air from the ocean rises toward the sky. Then, cool air begins swirling around the warm air. As water from the ocean is lifted into the air, a storm begins to form.

Compare and Contrast

Introduction

Hang large photographs of a cow and an alligator on the left and right sides of the board. Draw a large Venn diagram between them, labeling the parts *cow*, *both*, and *alligator*. Ask students to volunteer qualities that are the same or different, such as *They both have tails* or *The cow is black and white* and *the alligator is green*. Write *tails* under *both*, *black and white* under *cow*, and *green* under *alligator*. Introduce the term *compare and contrast*. Have students volunteer to write other descriptive words in the correct sections of the Venn diagram.

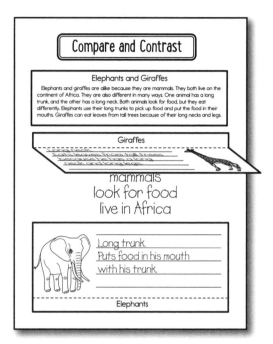

Creating the Notebook Page

Guide students through the following steps to complete the right-hand page in their notebooks.

1. Add a Table of Contents entry for the Compare and Contrast pages.

2. Cut out the title and glue it to the top of the page.

3. Cut out the *Elephants and Giraffes* passage and glue it below the title.

4. Read the passage.

5. Cut out the two flaps. Apply glue to the back of the top section of the *Giraffes* flap and the bottom section of the *Elephants* flap. Then, align the flaps so that they meet in the middle and attach the pieces to the page.

6. On each of the top flaps, use details from the text to tell how the giraffe and elephant are different. Then, open both flaps and write details from the text to tell what the two animals have in common.

Reflect on Learning

To complete the left-hand page, have each student draw a Venn diagram large enough to fill the page. Have students choose two animals to compare and contrast. Have them label the left and right circles with each of the animal's names and have them write *Both* above the inner circle. Provide resources for students to use in their research.

Compare and Contrast

Elephants and Giraffes

    Elephants and giraffes are alike because they are mammals. They both live on the continent of Africa. They are also different in many ways. One animal has a long trunk, and the other has a long neck. Both animals look for food, but they eat differently. Elephants use their long trunks to pick up food and put the food in their mouths. Giraffes can eat leaves from tall trees because of their long necks and legs.

Giraffes

_____

_____

_____

_____

Elephants

_____

_____

_____

_____

Making Inferences

Pack two small suitcases. Fill one with winter accessories such as mittens, a heavy coat, and boots. Fill the other with summer accessories such as sunscreen, a swimsuit, and sunglasses. Tell students that you are going on a trip and ask them to use clues to guess where you might be going and what you might do there. Open the suitcases one at a time. Entertain all guesses. Ask students how they came up with their guesses. When they point out the clues in the suitcases, tell them that stories and texts also offer clues to aid understanding. Introduce students to the term *inference*.

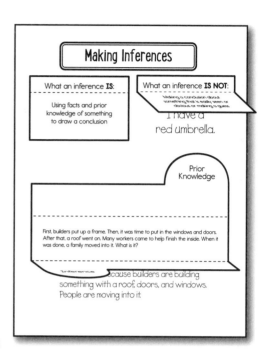

Creating the Notebook Page

Guide students through the following steps to complete the right-hand page in their notebooks.

1. Add a Table of Contents entry for the Making Inferences pages.

2. Cut out the title and glue it to the top of the page.

3. Cut out the *What an inference IS* flap. Apply glue to the back of the top section and attach it to the left side of the page below the title.

4. Cut out the *What an inference IS NOT* flap. Apply glue to the back of the top section and attach it beside the other flap.

5. Under the *What an inference IS* flap, write an example of an inference such as *My friend is wearing a fancy dress, so she is probably going to a party.* Then, under the *What an inference IS NOT* flap, write an example of an obvious statement such as *My friend is dressed up.*

6. Cut out the *Prior Knowledge* and *Inference* flap book. Apply glue to the back of the center section and attach it near the bottom of the page.

7. Read the text. Then, use details from the text to infer what the builders are building. Write your answer under the *Inference* flap. Explain how you inferred your answer. Then, under the *Prior Knowledge* flap, write how you used what you already knew to make your inference.

Reflect on Learning

To complete the left-hand page, have each student write a short paragraph about any topic. Tell students that one word should be a made-up word. Ask students to choose partners and exchange paragraphs. Partners should infer the meaning of the made-up words from their reading.

© Carson-Dellosa • CD-104653

Making Inferences

What an inference **IS**:	What an inference **IS NOT**:
Using facts and prior knowledge of something to draw a conclusion	Making a conclusion about something that is easily seen or obvious or making a guess

Prior Knowledge

First, builders put up a frame. Then, it was time to put in the windows and doors. After that, a roof went on. Many workers came to help finish the inside. When it was done, a family moved into it. What is it?

Inference

Fact and Opinion

Introduction

Ask students what they know about and think of penguins. Record their answers, which may include *black and white* or *funny,* on the board. Read a short article about penguins. Ask students to volunteer facts they just learned about penguins. Write them on the board as well. Then, draw a T-chart on the board. Label one side *Fact* and the other side *Opinion.* Discuss the difference. Return to the list of details describing penguins. Have students sort the details in the correct columns.

Creating the Notebook Page

Guide students through the following steps to complete the right-hand page in their notebooks.

1. Add a Table of Contents entry for the Fact and Opinion pages.

2. Cut out the title and glue it to the top of the page.

3. Cut out the *Fact* and *Opinion* pockets. Apply glue to the back of the left and right sides and the bottom of each pocket and attach them side by side to the middle of the page.

4. Complete the definitions of *fact* and *opinion.* (Fact: A statement that can be **proven**; Opinion: A **feeling** or **belief** about something)

5. Cut out the eight sentence strips. Read each one and decide if it is a fact or an opinion. Place each sentence strip in the correct pocket.

6. Write two more facts and two more opinions below the pockets.

Reflect on Learning

To complete the left-hand page, have each student write a short opinion piece on which type of animal is the best pet to own. Students should include some facts as well as their opinions. Have students highlight the facts and underline the opinions. Allow time for students to share their work.

Fact and Opinion

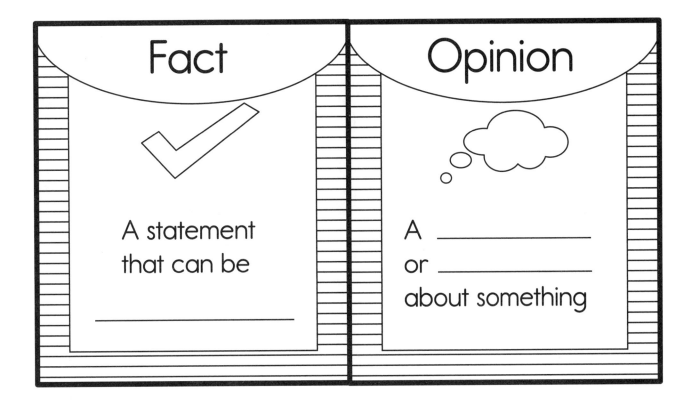

Fact

A statement that can be _____

Opinion

A _____ or _____ about something

Spiders have eight legs.	Valentine's Day is February 14.
Friday is the best day of the week.	Throwing a football is easy.
Chocolate is the best candy.	Spiders are scary.
There are seven days in a week.	A touchdown is worth six points in football.

Tabs

Cut out each tab and label it. Apply glue to the back of each tab and align it on the outside edge of the page with only the label section showing beyond the edge. Then, fold each tab to seal the page inside.

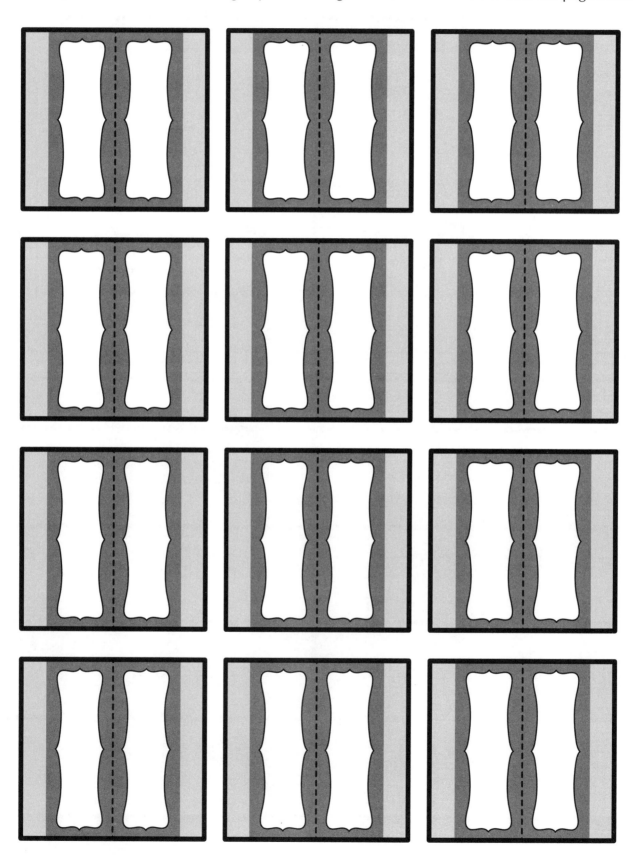

Cut out the KWL chart and cut on the solid lines to create three separate flaps. Apply glue to the back of the Topic section to attach the chart to a notebook page.

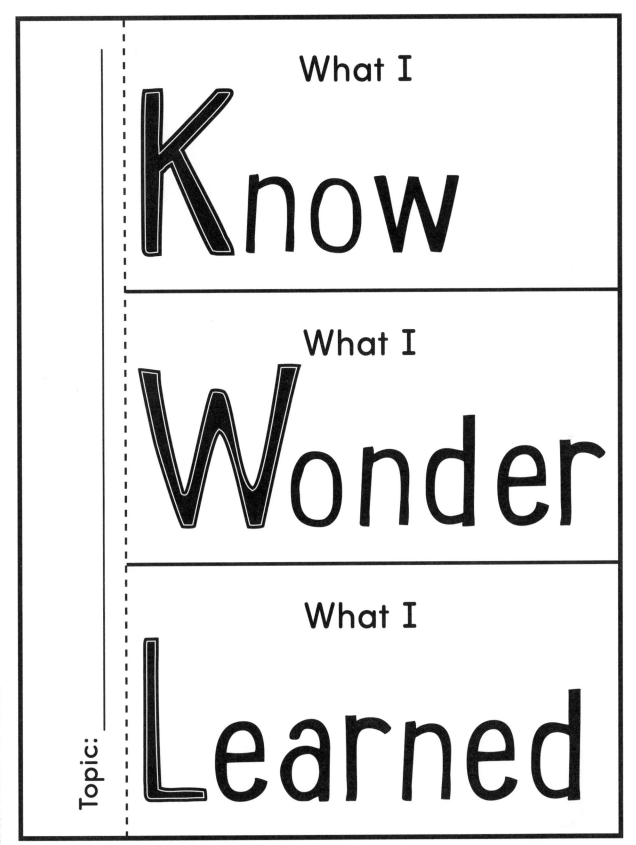

Library Pocket

Cut out the library pocket on the solid lines. Fold in the side tabs and apply glue to them before folding up the front of the pocket. Apply glue to the back of the pocket to attach it to a notebook page.

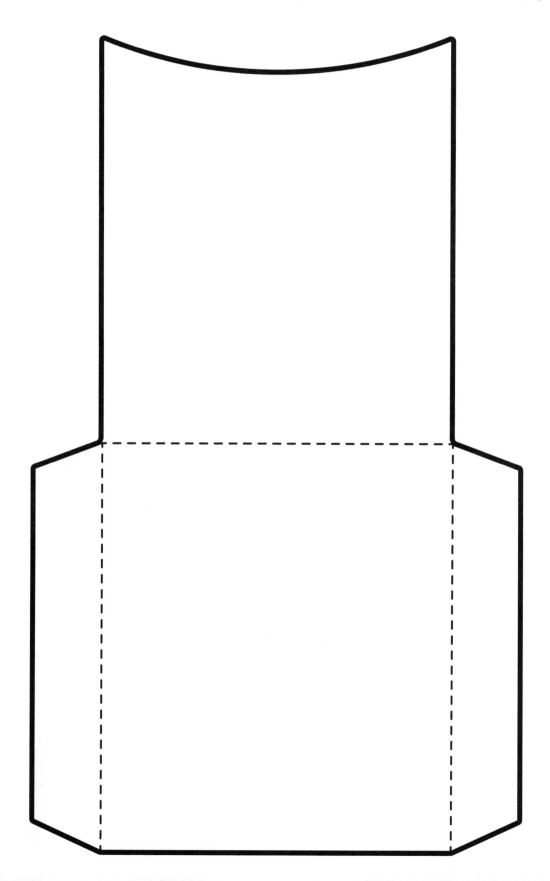

Envelope

Cut out the envelope on the solid lines. Fold in the side tabs and apply glue to them before folding up the rectangular front of the envelope. Fold down the triangular flap to close the envelope. Apply glue to the back of the envelope to attach it to a notebook page.

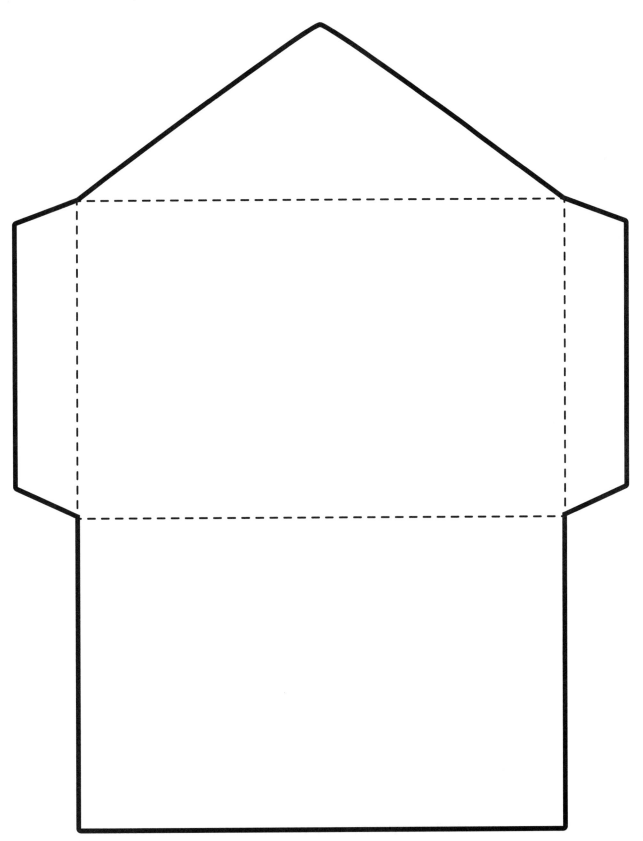

Pocket and Cards

Cut out the pocket on the solid lines. Fold over the front of the pocket. Then, apply glue to the tabs and fold them around the back of the pocket. Apply glue to the back of the pocket to attach it to a notebook page. Cut out the cards and store them in the envelope.

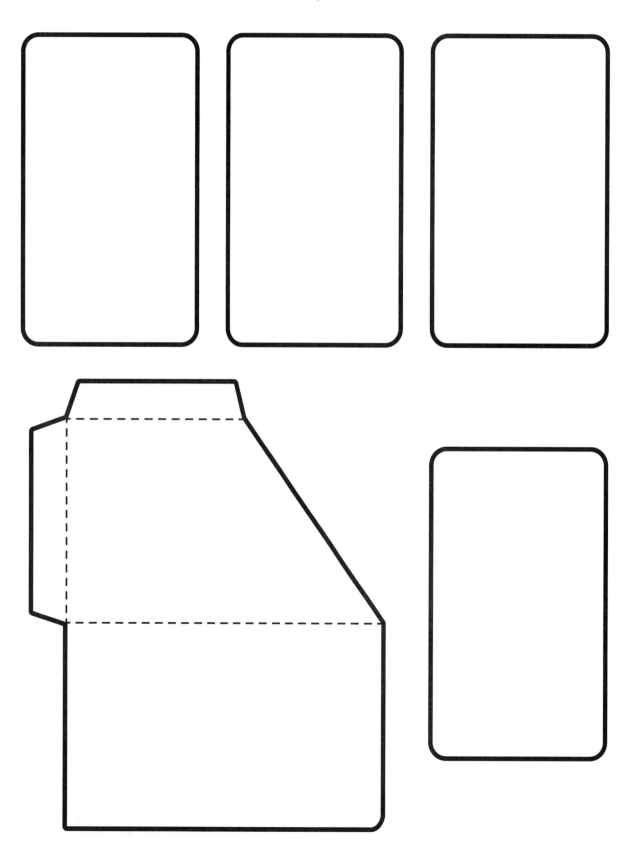

Six-Flap Shutter Fold

Cut out the shutter fold around the outside border. Then, cut on the solid lines to create six flaps. Fold the flaps toward the center. Apply glue to the back of the shutter fold to attach it to a notebook page.

If desired, this template can be modified to create a four-flap shutter fold by cutting off the bottom row. You can also create two three-flap books by cutting it in half down the center line.

Eight-Flap Shutter Fold

Cut out the shutter fold around the outside border. Then, cut on the solid lines to create eight flaps. Fold the flaps toward the center. Apply glue to the back of the shutter fold to attach it to a notebook page.

If desired, this template can be modified to create two four-flap shutter folds by cutting off the bottom two rows. You can also create two four-flap books by cutting it in half down the center line.

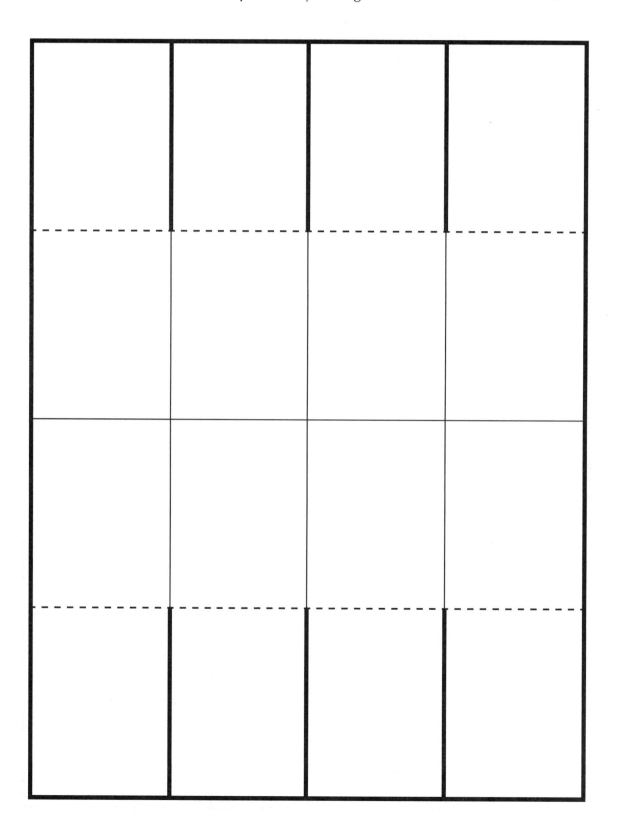

Flap Book—Eight Flaps

Cut out the flap book around the outside border. Then, cut on the solid lines to create eight flaps. Apply glue to the back of the center section to attach it to a notebook page.

If desired, this template can be modified to create a six-flap or two four-flap books by cutting off the bottom row or two. You can also create a tall four-flap book by cutting off the flaps on the left side.

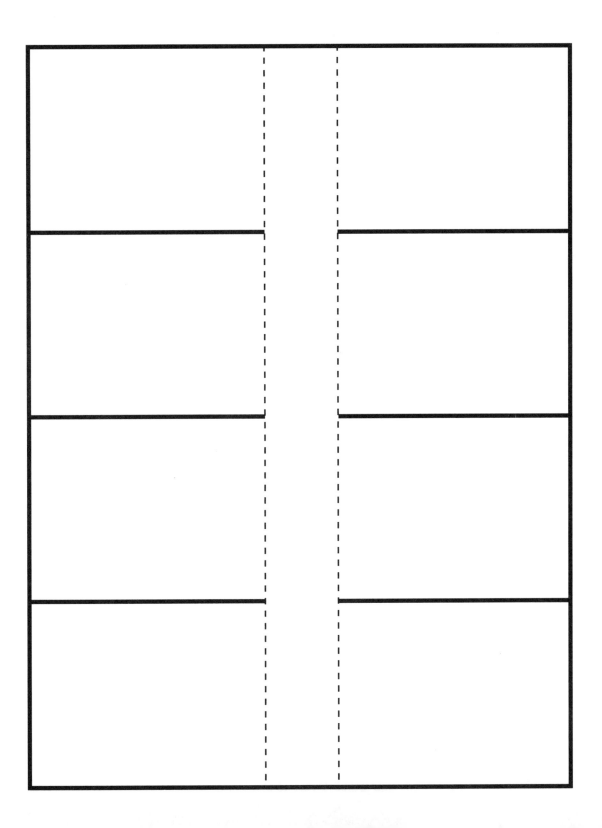

Flap Book—Twelve Flaps

Cut out the flap book around the outside border. Then, cut on the solid lines to create 12 flaps. Apply glue to the back of the center section to attach it to a notebook page.

If desired, this template can be modified to create smaller flap books by cutting off any number of rows from the bottom. You can also create a tall flap book by cutting off the flaps on the left side.

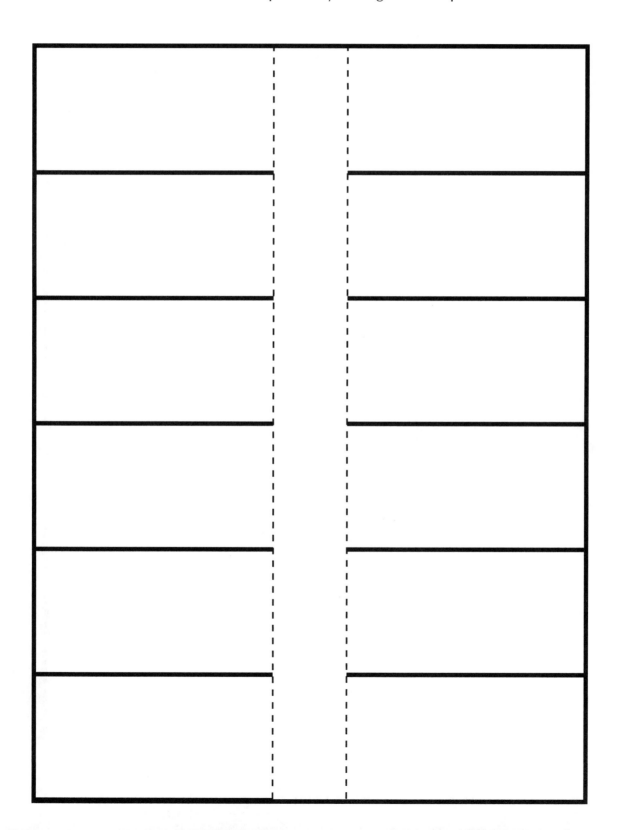

Shaped Flaps

Cut out each shaped flap. Apply glue to the back of the narrow section to attach it to a notebook page.

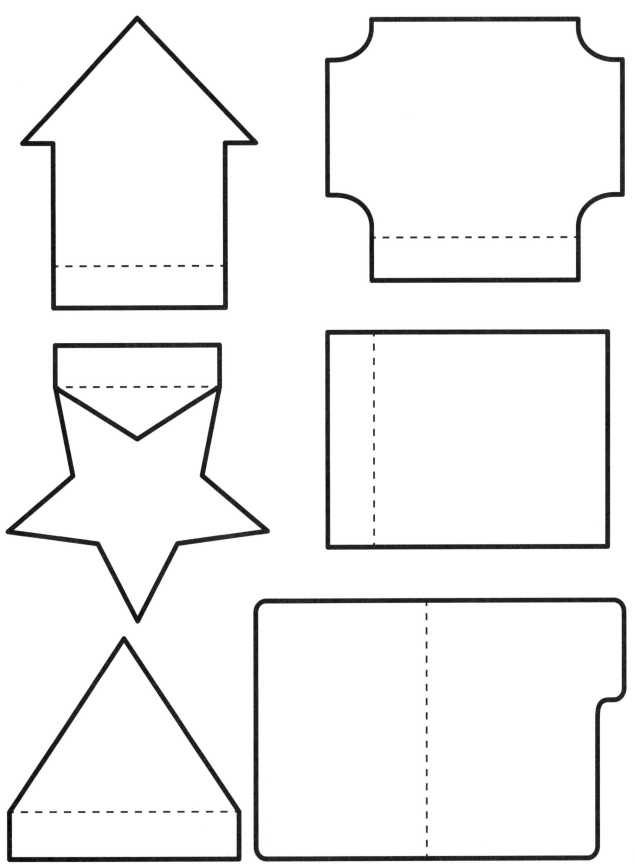

Shaped Flaps

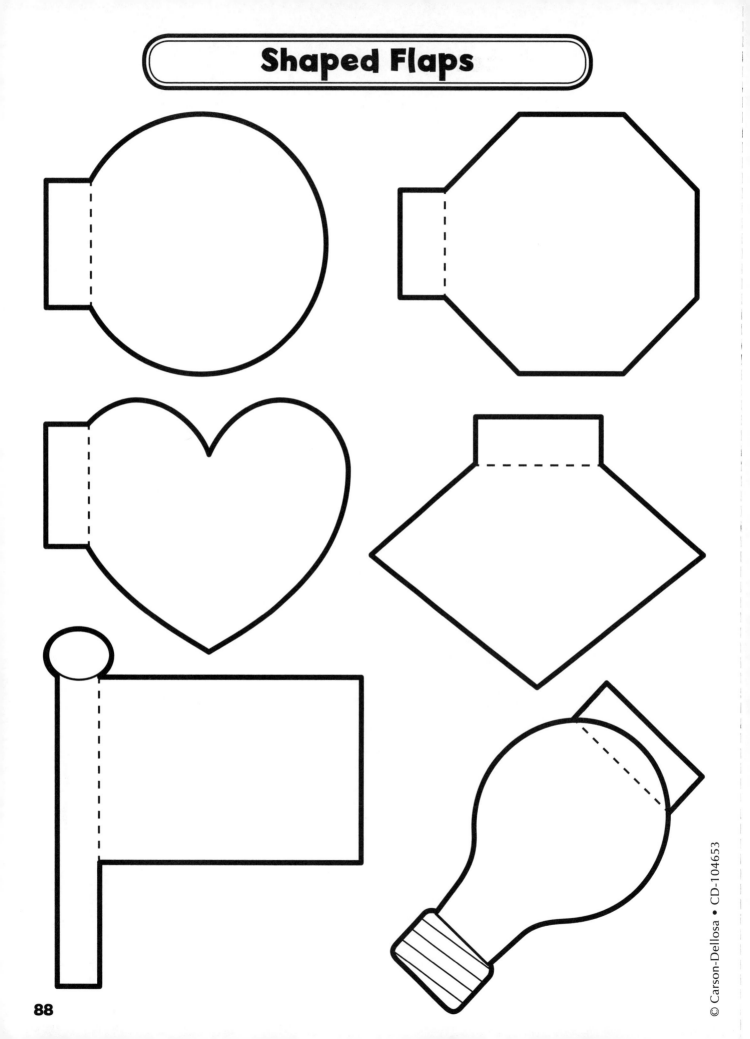

Interlocking Booklet

Cut out the booklet on the solid lines, including the short vertical lines on the top and bottom flaps. Then, fold the top and bottom flaps toward the center, interlocking them using the small vertical cuts. Apply glue to the back of the center panel to attach it to a notebook page.

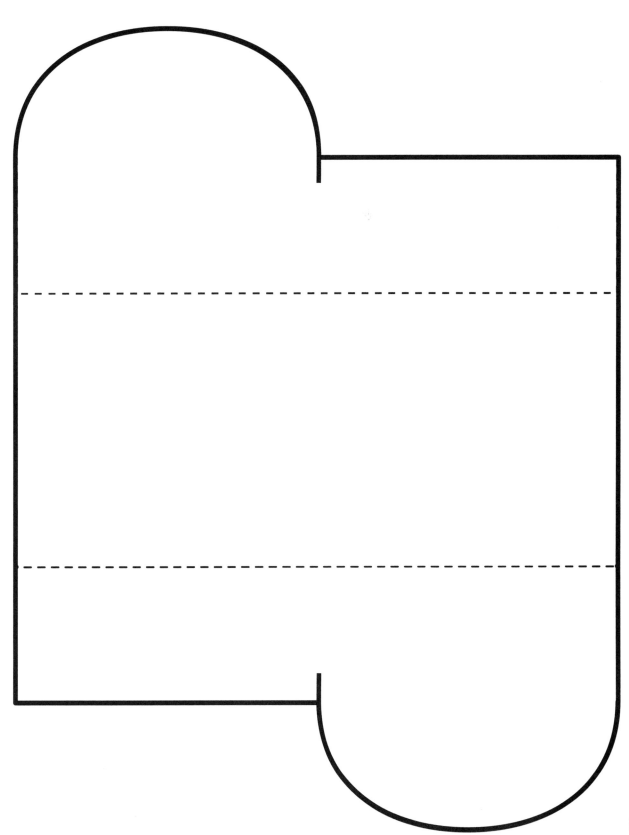

Four-Flap Petal Fold

Cut out the shape on the solid lines. Then, fold the flaps toward the center. Apply glue to the back of the center panel to attach it to a notebook page.

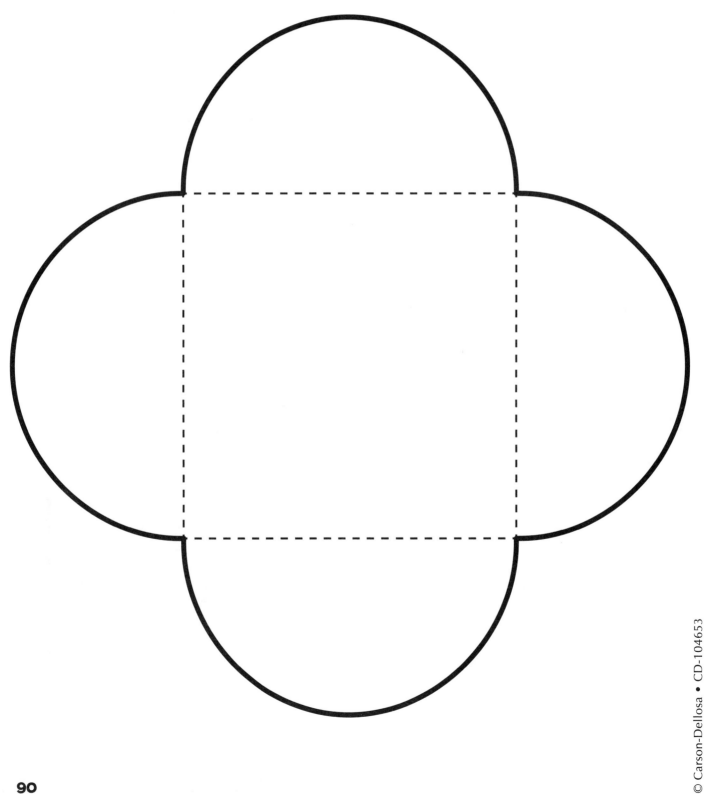

Six-Flap Petal Fold

Cut out the shape on the solid lines. Then, fold the flaps toward the center and back out. Apply glue to the back of the center panel to attach it to a notebook page.

Accordion Folds

Cut out the accordion pieces on the solid lines. Fold on the dashed lines, alternating the fold direction. Apply glue to the back of the last section to attach it to a notebook page.

You may modify the accordion books to have more or fewer pages by cutting off extra pages or by having students glue the first and last panels of two accordion books together.

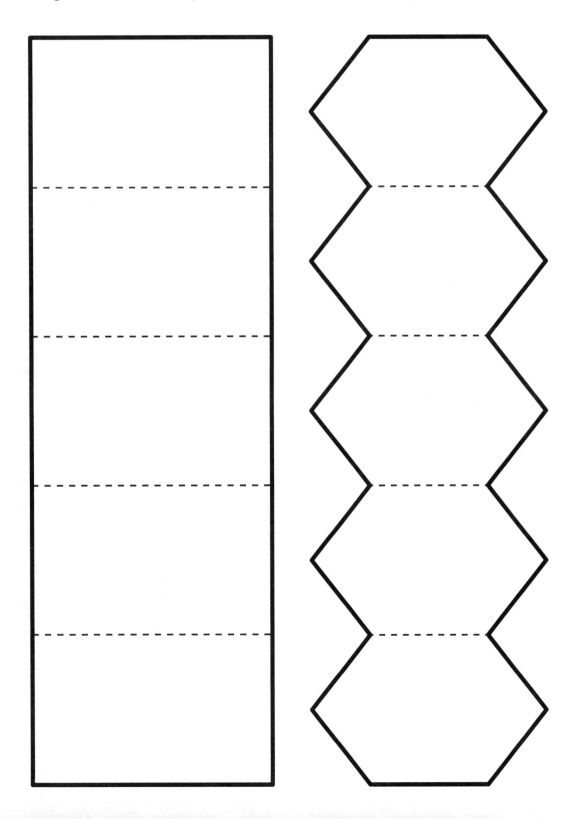

Accordion Folds

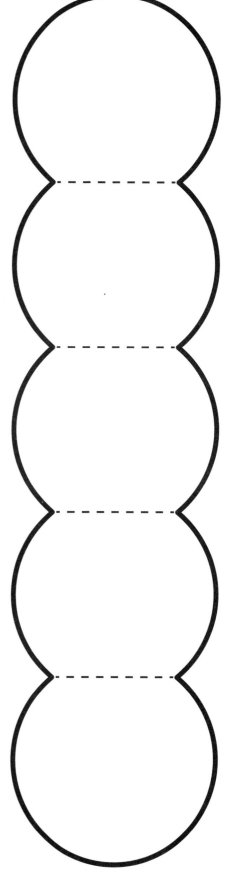

Clamshell Fold

Cut out the clamshell fold on the solid lines. Fold and unfold the piece on the three dashed lines. With the piece oriented so that the folds form an X with a horizontal line through it, pull the left and right sides together at the fold line. Then, keeping the sides touching, bring the top edge down to meet the bottom edge. You should be left with a triangular shape that unfolds into a square. Apply glue to the back of the triangle to attach the clamshell to a notebook page.

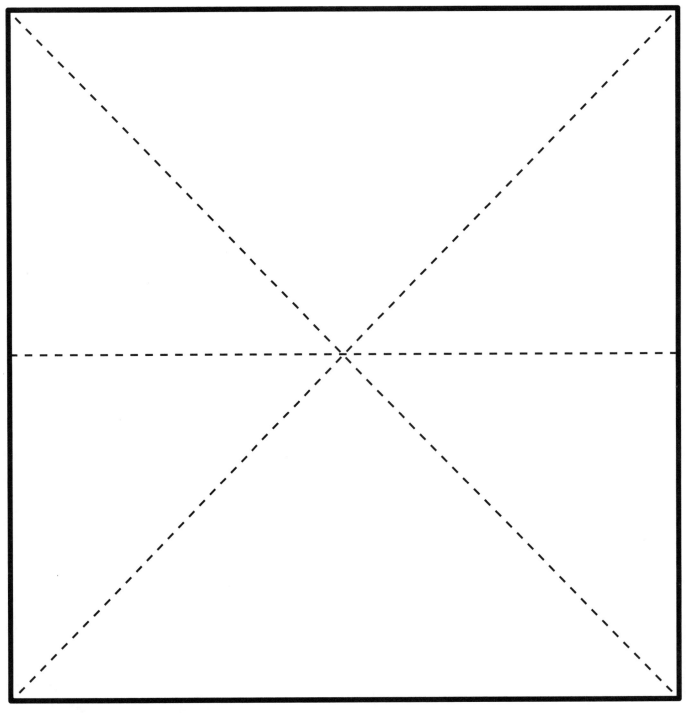

Puzzle Pieces

Cut out each puzzle along the solid lines to create a three- or four-piece puzzle. Apply glue to the back of each puzzle piece to attach it to a notebook page. Alternately, apply glue only to one edge of each piece to create flaps.

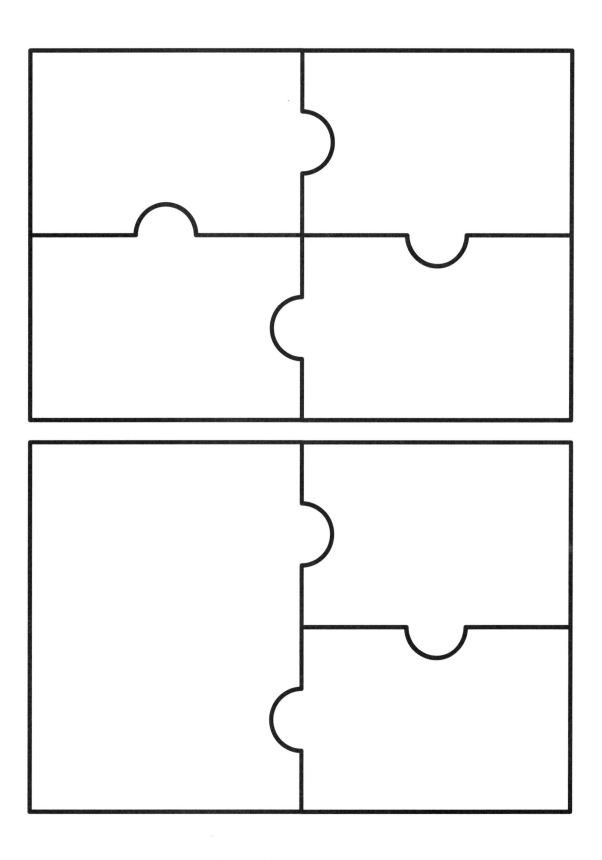

Flip Book

Cut out the two rectangular pieces on the solid lines. Fold each rectangle on the dashed lines. Fold the piece with the gray glue section so that it is inside the fold. Apply glue to the gray glue section and place the other folded rectangle on top so that the folds are nested and create a book with four cascading flaps. Make sure that the inside pages are facing up so that the edges of both pages are visible. Apply glue to the back of the book to attach it to a notebook page.

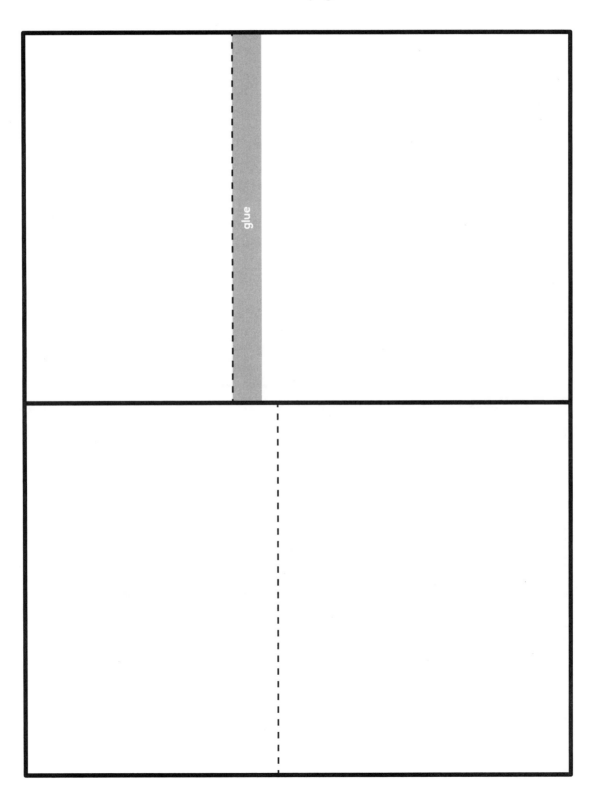

glue